A STRAIGHTFORWARD GUIDE TO BOOKKEEPING AND ACCOUNTS

TONY BANNISTER

Straightforward Publishing
www.straightforwardco.co.uk

Straightforward Guides
Brighton BN2 4EG

© Tony Bannister 2009

ISBN 9781847161147

Printed by GN Press Essex

Cover design by Bookworks Islington

CONTENTS

Introduction

Glossary of terms

Index

Introduction

In the current recession, the world is now a much tougher place for businesses and unfortunately many will fail. Apart from the fortunes of the market, the most common reasons are connected with what might be called sloppy management. Not paying attention to the routine but essential tasks can lead to the collapse of any business.

All businesses must therefore be managed, no matter what their size or complexity. Management means the control and co-ordination of all the constituent parts of a business - sales, purchases, production, distribution, credit, tax, etc. etc. A common denominator is therefore necessary to explain and clarify the whole range of business activities, and that common denominator is money.

Spending money and receiving money is a constant process and each transaction must therefore be reduced to a monetary expression and then recorded in a Book of Account. The process of recording all this information relating to the financial affairs of the business is Bookkeeping.

Financial management means keeping track of all money coming in and going out, whether cash or cheque, where it comes from, where it goes to, how long it takes, what is being purchased and what is being sold.

In addition to managing books and accounts, this book covers basic financial management, the formulation of budgets and management of cashflows. This builds on the actual recording of expenditure. Once the business manager has mastered the art of bookkeeping and accounts and formulation of budgets and monitoring of cashflow then the practice of business management will be that much easier and the prospects of survival that much greater.

Section 1

Bookkeeping and Accounts

1

The Books to Keep

Your business activities will consist of selling goods and/or services.

At the same time you will have to spend money on behalf of the business, on the purchase or rent of premises, raw materials, equipment, stationery etc. etc. in order to conduct business.

Remember that every business transaction generates a financial transaction, all of which must be recorded in books of account on an on-going basis. It is a fundamental management requirement that this be done on a regular basis, at a minimum once a week. Leave it much longer, and sooner or later an iron law of accounting will come into operation. You will have mislaid a financial record or simply forgotten to request one or issue one. When you do get around to up-dating the books, they won't balance. Unless you can discover the error before the end of the financial year your accountant will be faced with the task of reconciling "incomplete records", which he or she will enjoy because of the professional challenge but which costs you more money for more of his/her time.

What information must be kept?

As a minimum you must keep records of the following:

i) All the invoices raised (or rendered) on behalf of the business, either when the goods are delivered or the services supplied to you, or shortly afterwards. An invoice is a legal document and it constitutes a formal demand for money. It must provide enough information to identify the business which sent it, who it was sent to, what it is for and whether VAT is payable.

ii) A list of your Sales invoices numbered sequentially.

iii) All Purchase invoices received, and listed i.e. those demands made on your business for the payment of money.

iv) Wages and salaries paid, and to whom; Income tax and NI contributions paid over to the Tax authorities.

v) All chequebook stubs, paying-in slips/books, counterfoils of petty cash vouchers, business bank account statements. Without these you cannot compile your books of account.

vi) A full record of VAT, whether paid by or paid to the business.

The advantages of a bookkeeping system for your business

a) To provide accurate information sufficient to assess whether you are managing the business at a profit or a loss, or whether the business is solvent i.e. is there enough cash available in the business to pay all the outstanding liabilities on demand? The right information of the right kind at the right time is a vital management tool. Good management means making informed decisions of the right kind at the right time based on information that is true and therefore trustworthy.

b) To provide the information required for correct assessments of VAT and Income Tax, so as to avoid financial penalties (and possibly a suspect reputation) for incorrect and/or late payments. HM Revenue and Customs keep records for seven years and so must you. Your accountant will need the best information in order to minimise your tax liabilities, unless of course you decide to submit a statement of income to your Inspector of Taxes without recourse to an accountant. In any event the Inspector will require a calculation of your Income from the business in the form of an Income and Expenditure Account for each trading year.

c) To monitor the behaviour of the business over time by reference to financial summaries "at a glance". You don't need to remember for example how many meals were served in your restaurant business in this year compared with last year. The comparison that matters is the financial one with reference to the value of those transactions.

How to record the information you need

There are basically four methods of bookkeeping. Which one to choose will depend largely on the type and size of business you have established. Take advice from a business adviser or accountant if you are unsure as to which is the best one for your needs.

a) Proprietary systems.

These are best suited for sole traders in cash transaction types of business e.g. jobbing builders, market traders or some small shopkeepers. This type of business requires daily record keeping, often including till-rolls for the cash till and offers a simple method of control over finances. A number of pre-printed stationery systems are available at business bookshops. Select one that allows you enough space to record all that needs recording. Worked examples are set out at the beginning of each book to show you how to keep cash records and the bank position, which can be calculated by following the instructions included.

Cash businesses are more vulnerable than other types for the following reasons: -

i) It is far easier to lose or misplace paperwork. Therefore it is easier to lose control and lose money. Therefore it is more difficult to plan for the future.

ii) It is far more difficult to separate the cash that belongs in the business from the cash belonging to the proprietor.

iii) HMRC pay far closer attention to cash businesses because of the greater scope for "creative accounting" and tax evasion.
   To minimise these risks, cash business-proprietors are strongly advised to pay their daily cash takings into the bank by using pre-

printed paying-in books supplied by their bank. It is also vital to obtain receipts for purchases made from the takings and to keep them in an orderly fashion.

b) The Analysed Cash book System.

This is perhaps the most common method used by small businesses selling mostly on credit, with perhaps some cash sales. It relies on the single entry system of bookkeeping, where each entry is, as the name implies, made once only, and all entries are made in one book, the Cashbook. The analysed cashbook is the "bible" of the business. It allows "at a glance" analysis because it is arranged on a columnar basis, showing how much has been received into the business, when and from where, how much of each receipt is attributable to VAT and therefore how much is the net amount belonging to the business. All this information is written up on one side of a pre-printed book, the left-hand page, showing all monies paid into the bank on behalf of the business. On the opposite, right-hand page are set out in separate columns details of what has been spent by the business, in other words, monies paid out of the bank, to whom and when.

This system is explained and illustrated in greater detail later in this chapter.

c) The Double Entry System

This method of recording accounts relies on ledgers, or **separate books of account** for each type of transaction. Far greater detail and control are possible using this system. As well as a cash account there is scope for setting up other ledgers such as the bought ledger for purchases, sales ledger, nominal (or business expense) ledger, salaries and so on.

It is much easier to monitor how much has been spent over a period of time on each type of transaction, simply by referring to the particular ledger or account, on each of which a running balance is struck. Every transaction is recorded in the major account called the

Cash Account and also in the appropriate subsidiary ledger. In this way the Cash Account acts as a "Control" account for all the separate accounts of the business. The most important feature of this system is the characterisation of all bookkeeping entries as either a "credit" ("he trusts" i.e." the business owes him") or "debit" ("he owes"). The sophistication of this method lies in the use of two entries for each transaction. For each credit entry in the Cash Account there must be a corresponding debit entry for the same amount in a different account. Likewise for each debit entry in the Cash Account there must be a corresponding credit entry in a different account. The key words are "equal and opposite". That way the greatest possible degree of control is obtained. This system is explained and illustrated in greater detail further on in chapter 2.

d) Computerised Accounting Systems

A wide variety of off-the-shelf packages are available, which rely on single or double entry methods. It may be tempting to invest in an accounts package at the outset, especially if you intend to use other computer packages in the business. It would be most unwise to start using such a package without understanding the principles that underlie them. Businesses have failed because of the familiar - "GIGO" - garbage in, garbage out. Money is the lifeblood of the business so don't turn it into garbage by neglecting an understanding of the what, why and how of bookkeeping.

The single entry system and the analysed cashbook

You will need to record the following financial information - for the efficient management of the business and for your accountant, in order to prepare the accounts of the business at the year's end: -

i) monies coming into the business from all sources - Income from Sales and other kinds of Receipts not derived from Sales i.e. INCOME and RECEIPTS; and
ii) monies going out of the business to all destinations i.e. PAYMENTS and EXPENSES.

From these aggregate accounts can be ascertained the following:

- Value of sales per month
- Value of receipts from other sources
- Value of VAT

Looking at Income & Receipts first, consider the following information extracted from the Cashbook of "Daves Building Supplies", a sole proprietorship.

During the course of the month he recorded the following

Payments and Expenses

Date	Cheque no.	Details	£	Nov
02	00046	Freds Parts		96
03	00047	Sid's Fabrics		123
03	00048	British Telecom		95.99
12	00049	Lloyd's Bank: cash		100.0
12	00050	London Press		17.50
12	00051	Lloyd's: Petty cash		83.50
22	00052	Smart's Manufactures		10.75
25	00053	Green Agency: rent		300.0
28	00054	W H Smith		15.25
30	00055	Smart's Manufactures		115.0
30	00056	Joan Wilson: wages		85.00

Also in the same month he recorded the following

Income and Receipts

Date	Receipt no.	Details	£
04	23	Building Soc Transfer	400
09	24	Market takings (9 Nov)	204
09	25	S Jones Invoice 92	575

16	26	Market takings (15th Nov)	165
16	27	J Slade Inv 83	328
23	28	Market takings 23 Nov	30
29		Market takings 29 Nov	342
30	30	M Howes Inv 71	750
30	31	Market takings 30 Nov	210
30	32	A Smith Inv 98	115

These entries are set out in his Cash book for the month thus, showing how they are analysed, column by column:-

INCOME AND RECEIPTS
These entries always appear on the left-hand side of each page of the cashbook.

See Overleaf.

INCOME AND RECEIPTS

Date	Details	Folio	Total	Net Cash Sales	Net Invoice sales	Transfers	VAT
Nov 04	Building Soc Trf	23	400.00			400.00	
Nov 09	Market takings	24	204.00	173.62			30.38
Nov 09	S.Jones:Invoice 92	25	575.00		489.36		85.64
Nov 16	Market takings	26	165.00	140.42			24.58
Nov 16	J Slade Invoice	27	328.00		279.15		48.85
Nov 23	Market takings	28	301.00	256.17			44.83
Nov 30	Market takings	29	342.00	291.06			50.94
Nov 30	M Lowes Invoice	30	210.00	178.72			31.28
Nov 30	A Smith Invoice 98	31	115.00		97.87		17.13
			3390.00	1039.99	1504.68	400.00	445.33

First note the entry "Transfer from Building Society-   £400.00.

This shows a transfer from Dave's Personal account into the business - a transfer of Capital. It has been included to illustrate the fact that the business account is separate from his personal account. The business now "owes" Dave £400 (hopefully temporarily), presumably because of a perceived risk of overdrawing the business account. This situation could arise because:

i) entering up his books on a daily basis he therefore knew in advance that the business would dip into overdraft. He could not anticipate his market takings on later dates in the month and at the same time knew that he had to meet expenses on behalf of the business, as indicated in the illustration.

ii) alternatively he had received word from the bank forewarning him of an overdraft situation in his business account.

What has not been shown in the illustration is the "Balance brought forward" from the previous month. Had this been in substantial credit he may not have had to make the transfer from his own funds. It has been assumed that this was not the case in order to emphasise the importance of prudence in the management of what is substantially a cash business, dependent upon market trading for most of the income.

All entries in the cashbook need to be adequately identified. A transfer needs to be identified as a Loan in a "Transfer" column, if indeed it is such, in which case it will have to be repaid at a later stage. On the other hand it may be intended to be long-term, i.e. for more than a year, in which case it probably then represents a contribution of Capital to the business. The business again "owes" Dave £400, because we are dealing with two separate financial entities.

Notice the distinction made in two separate columns between "Cash sales" receipts and "Invoice sales" receipts for earlier sales made by granting credit to customers. This is made again because Dave's

Motors is a part credit/part cash business. By showing the two separately he is able to monitor the progress of the two kinds of trading. Apart from a natural "feel" he would undoubtedly develop for this aspect of his business he is able to prove it by reference to his cashbook.

By identifying the number of each invoice against payment he can cross-reference these payments to an Invoice Book, which simply lists all invoices raised, in consecutive number sequence. Upon payment of an invoice he can mark it off against his list, showing at a glance which remain outstanding, and which if any have been part-paid only.

The only other kind of Income or Receipt into the business, apart from sales, loans or capital contributions, would derive from the sale of unwanted physical assets such as second hand equipment.

Credit control

This is the term used for monitoring payments and comparing them against invoices still outstanding, which invoices reflect the amount of credit the business has granted to its debtors. The emphasis is on the word "Control". Without regular attention to this aspect of the business control will be more difficult to maintain and can eventually be lost.

So long as the bookkeeping is updated regularly Dave will know:

i) what invoices have been raised and who for;

ii) which have been paid, fully or in part;

iii) which remain outstanding;

iv) how long they have been outstanding;

v) how much he is owed by debtors of the business.

So long as he has this information and trusts it to be accurate he is in a position to make an informed decision about what he then needs to do about each outstanding invoice. He will also know just how much of the working capital of the business has been extended to debtors.

Returning to the cashbook, it can be seen at a glance how much has been received and what the individual amounts and the totals for the month represent. This is achieved simply by extending the arithmetical entry across the page and writing in the sum in the appropriate column.

EXPENSES/PAYMENTS

See overleaf

PAYMENTS AND EXPENSES

Date / VAT Cash	Details	Cheq No	Total	Stock	tel	Pub	Draw	Petty	Rent	Stat	Wages	Wages
Nov02	Freds parts	46	96	81.70								14.30
Nov02	SidsFabrics	47	123	104.68								18.32
Nov03	BT	48	95.99		81.69							14.30
Nov12	Lloydscash	49	100									
Nov12	Londonress	50	17.50			14.90						2.60
Nov12	Lloydscash	51	83.50				100	83.50				
Nov22	Smarts	52	10.75	9.15								1.60
Nov25	Agencyrent	53	300									
Nov28	WH Smiths	54	15.25									2.27
Nov28	Smarts	55	115	97.87					300			17.13
Nov30	Wages	56	85							12.98	85	
			1041.99	293.4	81.69	14.90	100	83.50	300	12.98	85	70.52

This side of the cashbook uses the same method of showing the total amounts paid, a referencing system based upon cheque numbers and extensions of the sums across the page into separate columns. The right hand side of the page is always used because there will always be a greater number of different destinations of payments than there will be for receipts, and all books are printed with more columns on the right hand side than on the left. All pre-printed books, and loose-leaf sheets, will follow this layout.

To avoid possible later confusion, and to maximise the information available to your accountant, enter as much information as possible in the "Details" or narrative column. Also remember to enter the date a cheque is drawn and the cheque number, in the respective columns, as shown. The number of columns used will obviously depend upon the complexity of the business and therefore the number of types of transaction that occur.

Always use a cashbook that contains more columns than you need for day-to-day transactions. Publishers of business accounts stationery produce a wide range of alternatives, from 2 column books to 42 column books. These are coded to indicate the number of columns, e.g. 5/14, 5/16 and 5/18 being among the most common ones sold. The first figure indicates the number of columns on the Receipts side of the page and the second figure, the number of columns on the Expenses/Payments side.

In the course of a trading year the majority of trading expenses will be those that have been anticipated, such as rent for premises. You may have attempted an estimate for other known heads of expenditure, such as telephones and postage, or the running costs of a delivery van. Although it can be difficult to estimate accurately how much will be spent on each head, you should be able to identify the types of expenditure you know will be incurred. If you are unsure about this then your accountant can advise. Do not sail into a business venture without first doing your homework!

Note particularly the following division of expenses into Non-trading and trading expenses: -

A) Non-Trading Expenses

Capital Equipment
In the cashbook you need to record expenditure on any non-trading expense, i.e. capital items such as machinery or computer equipment. The purchase price of such items must be recorded separately from any running costs, even though all financial outlays of whatever kind are recorded in the cashbook as expenses.

Non-trading expenditure does not form part of the Profit & Loss account, and is recorded by convention in the final column of the cashbook. This column can be identified as e.g. "Capital", or "Sundries", and an adequate note made alongside the entry to explain what each entry represents.

B) Trading Expenses
All heads of expenditure connected with running the business are Trading Expenses, including VAT.

Aggregated, they form one section of the equation needed to calculate the profit or loss at the end of the financial year. They are examined more fully in chapter 5, which deals with the Final Accounts, one of which is the Profit & Loss Account. The other part of the Final Accounts is called the Balance Sheet.

As well as regular anticipated types of expense there will sometimes be irregular expenditure on anticipated items of a non-capital nature, possibly occurring only once in a trading year. These would include Insurance premiums, if paid annually. Accordingly there might be a column kept open for "Insurances". A similar case arises with Business Rates, which are payable either in one annual amount or in 10 equal instalments. More regular heads of expense might include some of the following, for each of which a separate column will be needed:

Salaries and Wages
It is the norm to pay salaries and wages by BACS. Wages can be

recorded separately in a Wages Account book so long as they are also entered in the cash book, especially if they are paid on a regular basis. Always identify in the Details column the name of the person(s) you pay, for ease of reference to your Wages Book.

Naturally you will have to pay Income Tax and National Insurance contributions, as deducted from gross salaries/wages. Such payments will be recorded in separate columns, which are not shown in the example.

Rent

Payments of Rent should also include the time period to which it refers, e.g. the month or the quarter year.

VAT

The "Total" column for each payment shows the gross figure as is recorded on the cheque stub, and includes any VAT. If you are registered for VAT then this can be reclaimed. VAT must be separately accounted for. Accordingly there must be a column to show the VAT element of the expenditure. VAT is dealt with in chapter 7. Briefly, if your aggregated Turnover i.e. sales income, reaches or is expected to reach a prescribed threshold level during the course of the year then you must register for VAT. Because the rate is at a high level (currently 15% although probably rising again to 17.5% by the end of 2009) it is a significant proportion of the cash flowing in and out of a business.

Petty Cash

You will almost certainly need to spend small sums of cash, often on a daily basis, on behalf of the business. These payments are quite separate from your own personal cash expenditure on such trivia as clothes, entertainment or food for the weekend.

Petty cash for the business is drawn from the bank by cheque in the same way as any other item of expense, as shown in our example. Petty Cash is dealt with more fully in chapter 6.

Drawings

Apart from monies flowing in and out of the business as a consequence of trading and recorded in the cash book, it should not be forgotten that the whole purpose of the exercise is to provide you, the owner, with a living. Since the business is likely to be your sole source of personal income, you will need to withdraw income from it during the course of trading for the purposes of meeting your personal commitments. You cannot live on nothing until the end of the financial year in anticipation of enough profit from the business for the preceding 12 months. Drawings will be offset against the profits of the business, as calculated at the end of the business financial year and declared to HMRC.

The "Drawings" column shows the amounts of money drawn out from the business i.e. paid to the proprietor by the business. Therefore it constitutes a business "expense" just as clearly as any other item of business expense, such as wages or salaries paid to employees. It is not however to be confused with these because the owner of the business (i.e. you) is not an "employee" of the business if it is a sole trader or a partnership. You might become an employee of your own business only if it is set up as a Limited Company.

In summary, every expense incurred by the business is entered into the Expenses/Payments side of the cash book. These include payments for purchases of materials and/or stock, bought for re-sale by the business.

Payments are arranged in columns to group together types of purchase, for the purposes of control and analysis.

At the end of a period of trading, monthly, quarterly, half-yearly and annually, it is then a straightforward exercise to calculate on-going costs, type by type. Following the reconciliation of the cashbook to the bank at the end of each month, thereby proving the accuracy of the bookkeeping entries, the "bottom line " figures are then transferred forward to become the opening balances for the subsequent month.

24

2

The Accounts to Keep

Technically speaking, "Bookkeeping" means the recording of business transactions in Books of Account.

"Accounting" means taking financial information from the books of account and using it to explain and understand the financial position of the business.

This chapter explores more fully the relationship between the two functions, by introducing the Double Entry system of bookkeeping and the creation of accounts maintained separately from the cash account.

The Double Entry System

This method is fundamentally different to the Single Entry/Analysed Cash book system in which, as we have seen, all financial transactions are recorded in one book of account.

Nevertheless, the Double Entry method follows the same procedures of money management as in the single entry/cash book method. Payments into the bank of cash and cheque are made the same day of receipt, and all payments out of the business are made by cheque or by cash from petty cash.

Using this method, one account, called the "Cash Account", is used to record all banking entries i.e. all monies received into and all cheque payments for monies going out of the business. The Cash Account therefore acts as what can be called a "Control Account". All other entries can be related back to the Cash Account for checking and control purposes.

As noted in chapter 1 this is because for every entry made in the Cash Account a second equal and opposite entry for the same amount must be made in a separate account. The Double Entry system also relies upon each entry being either a Credit or Debit entry. Credit means "he owes" (to the business), and Debit means "he trusts", (i.e. the business owes him). So the second leg of the system works as noted also in chapter 1. For every credit entry in the Cash Account the corresponding entry in the other account must be a debit. Likewise, for every debit entry in the Cash Account the corresponding entry in the other account must be a credit.

This explains how the internal control mechanism works within the business.

All Cash Account entries are reflected in banking entries, which are shown eventually on the bank statements of the business. The bank therefore acts as the External "Control" account for the business, as seen from the Cash Account.

Since the bank also employs the Double entry system of recording its accounts with its customers, the double entry system operates between the bank and the Cash account of your business.

It therefore follows that for every credit entry in your cash account the corresponding entry in the Bank's account of the business must be a debit entry. Likewise for every debit entry in your cash account the corresponding entry in the Bank's account of the business must be a credit entry.

Every time you receive a cheque or cash in payment for the supply of goods and/or services, you pay it into the bank on behalf of the business. On the bank statement that is eventually received, such payments are recorded by the bank as "Credits".

Therefore, and according to the double entry system of bookkeeping, the corresponding entries for payments received must be recorded in the Cash account as "Debits". Paradoxical but logical.

Looking at the relationship between any entry shown on the bank statement and the same entry shown in an internal account, it follows that these will be identical, as to whether they are Credits or Debits, since the account "in between" (the Cash Account) will be the opposite.

To take a simple example from the illustration of a business in the previous chapter – Dave's Motors.

He sells some parts to an existing customer on credit and then receives payment by cheque. He pays the cheque into the bank and the entry shows up on the bank statement the following week as a Credit, since he now has more money in the bank than previously. The corresponding entry on his Cash account must therefore be a Debit entry for cash received, according to the double entry method.

A Debit entry on his Cash account therefore requires a corresponding Credit entry on another internal account, in this case the account of the customer and identified as such e.g. Dave's Motors A/c.

Again if he buys stationery on credit, his stock of stationery increases, as does its monetary value, and the amount that he owes to the supplier increases by a corresponding amount. One entry is shown as a credit and the other as a debit. It is unwise to attempt to set up a double entry system of bookkeeping without having understood the fundamental theoretical and practical essentials. Many people possess all the necessary entrepreneurial and product knowledge skills for success in business. At the same time many retain a mild (or severe) phobia of bookkeeping, accounts and all things to do with numbers. Hopefully by now any phobias have been alleviated, if not dispelled. Whichever system you use, your books will form the basis of the Final Accounts of the business, which are dealt with later on in the book.

TYPES OF ACCOUNT

Accounting convention requires that all internal accounts be classified according to the following description: -

1) Personal Accounts

These record transactions with particular customers, i.e. those with whom the business regularly deals. A separate customer account is kept in the name of each customer.

2) Nominal Accounts

These record the Expenses incurred in running the business and the Income generated from sales. Again a separate account is maintained for each type of expense, e.g. electricity, business rates, stationary, telephones, postage etc. Likewise separate accounts are also kept for income from different sources.

3) Real Accounts

These accounts are kept for assets and their different types, e.g. office furniture, computer equipment, vehicles etc.

Such accounts are sometimes referred to as "Ledgers", as an alternative mode of description. With every type of account - Personal, Nominal or Real, each financial transaction is recorded in the separate sub-account to which it relates as well as in the main Cash account.

Accounts can be illustrated as follows:

NAME OF ACCOUNT

Date	Details/Narrative	Debit	Credit	Balance

FURNITURE AND FITTINGS ACCOUNT

Date	Details/narrative	Debit	Credit	Balance
Nov 1	Cash A/C	400.00		(400.00)

TELEPHONE ACCOUNT

Date	Details/Narrative	DR	CR	Balance
Nov 3	Cash A/C	142.00		(142.00)

28

CASH ACCOUNT

```
-----------------------------------------------------------Date
Details/Narrative      DR      CR    Balance
-----------------------------------------------------------
Balance b/fwd                        (3400.00)

Nov 1   Furn/Fittings A/C        400.00   3000.00
Nov 3   Telephones A/C           142.00   2858.00
```

And so on and so on, creating a separate account for each type of expense, and making corresponding entries on the Cash account for each entry made on a named account.

A useful way to treat bookkeeping is to view it as a special language, with its own unique vocabulary and rules of grammar. One common rule is that the term Credit is often abbreviated to CR, and Debit abbreviated to DR, as shown above.

Furthermore, it is a fundamental rule that all accounts show Debit entries on the left-hand side and Credit entries on the right hand side. All bank statements adhere to the same convention. A simple way to remember this is that there is an "R" in Credit and an "R" in Right, so "Credits go on the Right, right?" All accounts fit into one of four different categories, as follows

1) INCOME.

2) EXPENSES.

3) ASSETS. Examples include: Furniture; Vehicles; Buildings; Leases; Computers; Stock; Cash in hand; Cash at bank; Work in Progress (part finished products); Debtors (Customers who have not yet paid for goods/services supplied/delivered).

Assets are in fact what is "Owned" by the business, at any particular time.

4) LIABILITIES

These describe what the business "Owes" to others, and include:

Trade Creditors: those suppliers owed money by the business for goods/services already supplied/delivered but not yet paid for.

Accrued Expenses: expenses relating to the current period for which no invoice has yet been received from the supplier and for which payment is not yet due, but which you know will become payable in the future, e.g. a telephone account which straddles two accounting periods.

Bank Overdraft: The bank's money, which does not belong to the business and will have to be repaid, either on demand or on a negotiated date.

Assets and liabilities will be collated and appear as the Balance Sheet of the business, and will include one other figure from the second main account, the Profit and Loss Account.

This will be either the profit or loss of the business for the period, calculated by subtracting the aggregate Expenses from the aggregate Income for the same period.

This is because a profit represents an additional amount of capital available to the business and a loss represents a reduction in the amount of capital available. In any event, all capital items and changes to the capital used in the business are displayed in the Balance Sheet.

This equation can be illustrated as follows:-

INCOME
a)   minus EXPENSES

= PROFIT or LOSS

b)   ASSETS +PROFIT/-LOSS
        minus LIABILITIES

   = NET ASSETS
   _____

These equations represent the basic formulae for calculating the overall financial position of the business, utilising every single account, or ledger, referred to earlier in the four categories. These formulae will be elaborated upon in the course of chapter 4 (the Final Accounts).

To compile the Profit and Loss Account and the Balance Sheet requires a simple exercise of collating all the closing balances on all the accounts at the end of the Accounting Period (the financial year of the business) and arranging them into their appropriate categories.

Below are a few examples of important adjustments to accounts that may need to be made in order to provide accuracy.

DEBTORS

Is the term used to describe those who owe money to the business. Debtors represent an asset of a business and therefore appear only in the Balance Sheet. You will have adopted one of two methods to record and monitor the situation with debtors.

a) You may have "lumped" them all together in one aggregate Debtors Account; or

b) Separated them out into named Debtor accounts, so as to more closely monitor the comparative progress of each and to maintain closer control of the most important. At the end of the year, in order to compile a summary of debtors, you will need to collate the final balances on each separate account to arrive at an aggregate Debtors account.

BAD AND DOUBTFUL DEBTS

At the end of the year there will almost certainly be customers who have not paid what they owe when the Final Accounts are compiled. Some of those debts will be paid during the course of the following financial year. But you may have doubts as to whether they will all be paid in full, or when.

Are there some debts which are very old and about which you are unsure about eventual payment?

Have you spent time and effort in fruitless attempts at recovery?

Have you gone so far as to instruct Solicitors to commence legal proceedings for recovery?

Have any of the debtors of the business become insolvent/"disappeared"?

If the answer to any of these questions is yes, or possibly, or probably, then either a bad or a doubtful debt has arisen. You will have to take a view as to which outstanding debts fall into each category because you will need to make separate provisions for each in the final accounts.

Many business people are reluctant to take firm action for recovery of either a sum outstanding or for the return of goods supplied. Many others will take whatever action they deem necessary to effect recovery of one or the other. In any event it is not possible to effect the return of a service rendered, for the obvious reason that nothing tangible can be physically recovered.

Whether to try for recovery or not is a practical decision, governed by the circumstances of the time and the inclination of the proprietor.

In the accounts, successful recovery of a debt means that the Debtors account must be reduced, because the cash in hand or cash at the bank will have been increased. Successful recovery of the goods means once again that the Debtors account must be reduced, because the Stock account will have been increased. The double entry system at work - any credit to one account must be matched by a corresponding debit to another account.

If neither the debt nor the goods can be recovered then the remaining option is to cut your losses and write-off the debt from the books. In this case the sum becomes a bad Debt and must be treated in the appropriate way.

First the bad debt must be transferred from the Debtors account, since it is no longer an asset, to a Bad Debt account.

Since Bad debts will be shown as DR or Debit entries, it follows that the entries to reduce the Debtors account will be CR or Credit entries, in accordance with the double entry rules.

Bad debts are those you are sure will not be paid, nor any goods recovered, in all probability because the debtor has gone out of business or, formally or informally, you have been told you wont be paid.

Bad Debts by definition do not appear on the Balance Sheet because they have been removed from the Debtors account.

The write-off does appear in the Profit and Loss account as a Bad Debt Expense because it is an Expense or cost that the business has incurred in the current period.

Doubtful debts are different. They are by implication those you are not sure about.

Again the procedure is to create a special account by transferring doubtful debts to a "Doubtful Debt Provision Account". The balance on this account will be shown separately as set-off (or subtracted from) the Debtors account in the Balance Sheet, which will then indicate the net amount believed to be collectable.

Any provision for doubtful debts will also appear as an item in the Profit and Loss account as a "Doubtful Debt Provision", as an Expense, because it represents an anticipated though not yet proven Expense that will be borne by the business. Again, like the Bad Debt account, a Doubtful Debt Provision account will show DR or Debit entries, according to the double entry rules.

Dishonoured cheques

It is possible that these will occur from time to time and may eventually turn out to be either bad or doubtful debts. Until the situation is clearer, upon re-presentation and clearance through the banking system, these are best taken out of the books altogether. This is effected simply by reversing the entries already made to the cash account and in the other corresponding account.

Depreciation of assets

This is a technical subject best left to your accountant to calculate. Briefly it refers to the process of writing-off a proportion of the value of physical assets every year of their useful life, to reflect the fact that the assets will be "used up" over a period of years. The Book Values will eventually diminish to zero, even if assets are still in use.

It is beyond the scope of this book to explain the different methods and tax implications of Depreciation. Suffice it to say that it is shown in the Profit and Loss account as an Expense, or annual "cost" to the business, and also in the Balance Sheet as a set-off or subtraction from the original value of each asset.

In the Balance Sheet however both annual depreciation and depreciation "Accumulated" over each asset's lifetime is shown, to calculate the current, book value, or net worth of each asset. Further refinements relate to the treatment of Capital introduced into the business by the proprietor and to Drawings out of the business by the proprietor.

These issues will be dealt with more fully in chapter 5. At this stage, to complete the introduction, it is sufficient to remind ourselves that Capital is always treated as an Asset, and therefore appears as a Balance Sheet item, while Drawings are a specific form of Expense to the business and therefore appear in the Profit and Loss account.

3

The Trial Balance

The trial balance is simply a listing of all the final balances on all the Nominal accounts, both CRs and DRs. It may be produced periodically, monthly or quarterly, as well as at the end of the financial year. As well as providing the raw material for the preparation of Final Accounts, it is a simple but effective way to check the arithmetical accuracy of the books.

A typical Trial Balance format might look as follows:-

	DRs £	CRs £
* Amounts owed by customers	3000	
Cash at bank(Cash account)		2500
Petty Cash		60
* Administrative Expenses	1200	
Computer Equipment	2000	
* Furniture & Fittings	2000	
* Sales		6800
Creditors		460
Capital		3500
	8200	13320

Balances marked by a * are aggregate totals of all subsidiary accounts comprising that category.

i) Amounts owed by customers is another expression for Debtors. The figure shown could be made up from a large number of individual debtors, for which a subsidiary list would look as follows:

	DRs	CRs
J Smith	350	
C Brown	704	
F White	811	
etc	x	
etc	x	
etc	x	
	3000	

Similarly

ii) Administrative expenses:

	DRs	CRs
Postage	98	
Telephones & Fax	246	
Stationery	321	
Printing	47	
Travel expenses	211	
etc	x	
etc	x	
etc	x	
	1200	

Other accounts might also be shown as composites figures. The deciding factor will be the degree of complexity of the account. There is no absolute rule.

ii) The Sales account figure, taken from the Sales Ledger, will almost certainly represent the aggregate of a number of subsidiary sales accounts because it is simply best practise for control purposes to separate individual customer accounts.

These examples are used to illustrate the principles of the Trial Balance. So long as DR balances and CR balances are correctly identified as such then the process of extraction at the end of a period is straightforward. Should you need a reminder of the double entry system refer again to chapter 2. Remember that the Bank account acts as the "Control" account between the business and the bank, and that the Cash account acts as the "Control" account to all other internal accounts opened and maintained during the course of business.

There must be a corresponding DR on the Cash account for every CR entry shown on the Bank Statement and a corresponding CR entry on the Cash account for every DR on the Bank Statement.

For every CR entry on the Cash account there must be a corresponding DR entry on another internal account and for every DR entry on the Cash account a corresponding CR on another internal account--somewhere!

Therefore the total of all the CR balances must equal the total of all the DR balances. If the DRs total on the Trial Balance equals the CRs total then you have "proved" that the accounts are accurate, is that not so?

Well, not necessarily!

The mathematical laws of probability suggest that when dealing with a large enough number of similar tasks, sooner or later an error will be made. This is a polite way of saying that nobody is perfect, and no bookkeeper was ever perfect. There could be errors that are not revealed in a Trial Balance, which do not alter the fact that it balances.

Before looking at the more common types of error it is worth stating that as a starting point, if the Trial Balance does balance it is strong though not conclusive evidence that all the entries are correct.

Types of Error

The most common types of accounting error are as follows:

a) Errors of Omission. This describes the situation where a transaction is completely missing from the books, because not all the necessary entries have been made. This could arise because of oversight, or because there is no paperwork available to prompt the bookkeeping.

b) Errors of Commission. Occur where entries are made, but in the wrong accounts, e.g. a sale of £35 is made to J Smith but entered in the account of B Smith.

c) Errors of Principle. Occur where entries are made in the wrong type of account, e.g. a prepayment expense (payment of an expense account in advance of the period to which it relates), which is an asset, is incorrectly entered as an accrual (an expense item for the current period for which no invoice has yet been received, which is a liability.

d) Compensating errors. Two or more errors which, taken together, cancel each other out. If in the illustration Petty Cash, £60, had been overlooked and omitted altogether from the list of DRs, and Creditors had been incorrectly totalled to read £400, not £460, the total DRs would still equal the total CRs, but this time £10700 in each case.

e) Errors of Original Entry. Occur where the original figure entered is incorrect on both the CR and the DR sides of different accounts, e.g. a credit sale of £132 to B Brown is entered in both the Sales account and the Debtors account as £123.

f) Reversal of entries. Occurs where the correct accounts are used but both entries are made on the wrong side, e.g. where the Sales account is debited and the Debtors account is credited, instead of vice versa.

Other possible errors include errors of addition, or only entering one half of a transaction, i.e. omitting to make either a CR or DR completely. Such errors would be revealed by a Trial Balance exercise unless compensatory errors had been made to conceal them.

Even though the Trial Balance is not a foolproof method of checking for accuracy it is the best one available for the small business proprietor using the double entry system, provided it is produced on a regular basis and with the necessary attention to detail. If the book-keeping has been accurate throughout the accounting period the total CRS on the books will equal or balance the total DRs, so because the system is self-balancing the scope for not finding errors is much reduced.

The golden rules to remember when discovering an error are firstly to identify what type of error it is and secondly whether the necessary adjustment requires a corresponding adjustment to another account as well.

4

The Final Accounts

The Distinction between Capital and Revenue

All income received and all expenditure incurred by a business must be accounted for as either Capital or Revenue.

Capital

Simply put, Capital comprises the total of all kinds of wealth in a business used to produce Income. In the accounts, Capital must therefore be maintained intact, separate from other kinds of finance and clearly identified, showing losses or increases.

Revenue

All other accounts record Revenue items, which are either income or expenditure, showing the day-to-day transactions of the business. As we have seen, the difference between income and expenditure is either a profit or a loss. Profits can be withdrawn from the business, while losses represent reductions to available Capital.

To successfully stay in business you have to sell sufficient goods/services to generate:

i) enough revenue with which to carry on the business, ie cover the costs of running it; and
ii) a profit from which to draw out money to meet your personal living expenses; and
iii) perhaps enough additional profit to provide Capital to finance future growth, or to repay any capital loans from you and/or others to the business at the outset.

To successfully manage the business you need to know how all aspects of it relate to your sales, which is the underlying reason you keep accounts.

No matter how small or large your business is or becomes, you must know and monitor the following aspects of it;

i) The aggregate expenses of running it, over specific periods of time;

ii) The expenses in detail;

iii) How much money is tied up in stock and work-in-progress;

iv) What net profit is being made, period by period;

v) How much money is owed to the business;

vi) How much money is overdue for payment, and for how long;

vii) How much money is owed by the business and for how long.

All this information is revealed in the process of preparing a Trial Balance and in drawing up the Final Accounts.

Understanding what the books mean and keeping them up to date to reflect what has happened within it is vital for running it properly. Without well-kept books you cannot see where you've come from and if you don't know that you won't see where you are going. Incomplete or falsified books might fool you, but not your accountant nor the Tax authorities.

As we have seen, the two most important Final Accounts that either you or your accountant will prepare are:

i) The Profit and Loss Account; and

ii) The Balance Sheet.

Together these provide an historical record of the health and behaviour of the business, reduced to and expressed in terms of money.

THE PROFIT AND LOSS ACCOUNT

This subject was introduced in chapter 2 and, as the description implies it shows at a glance how much profit has been made, from a calculation of the total Income from business activities minus the total expenditure incurred in running it. There will be special characteristics in the layout chosen that reflect the uniqueness of your particular business, but in essence all P/L accounts follow the same basic format. The Title Line is always set out as follows; the date chosen here is taken at random for illustration purposes. The heads of text used are among the more common ones encountered in a small business.

PETERS STATIONARY SHOP
PROFIT AND LOSS ACCOUNT FOR YEAR ENDED 31ST MARCH 2009

	£	£
INCOME		
Sales proceeds	X	Add
Closing work in progress	X	
Less Opening work in progress	(X)	
Bank interest receivable	X	
Less: Expenditure		
Administrative expenses	X	
Salaries/wages	X	
Business rates	X	
Light and heat	X	

Postage	X	
Telephones	X	
Stationary	X	
Etc		
Etc		
Add Accrued expenses	X	
Less Prepaid expenses	(X)	
Add Bad debts	X	
Add Depreciation of assets for year	X	(X)

	X	

NOTES

i) Closing-work-in-progress. At any one time you may have done work on orders which are not yet finished. This work therefore is "in progress" and represents income earned which has not yet been invoiced. It is recognised as such in the P/L account (and also shown in the Balance sheet as a Current asset). It has to be accounted for because ultimately you will be completing the work and receiving payment, so at the moment the accounts are produced (31st March), the business is "owed" the money. Therefore you need to show Closing work-in-progress as an addition to Sales (CR) and show the same figure in the Balance Sheet as a Current Asset (DR).

ii) Opening-work-in-progress is the work that was in progress at the end of the previous accounting year and therefore must be deducted from Sales income for the year shown in these accounts. This is because it would have been invoiced and turned into Income during the year, or have become a bad debt and dealt with elsewhere in the accounts. If it were not deducted from this year's income it would have been included twice.

iii) Salaries/wages and Light/Heat could be further separated out if there were substantial sums involved.

iv) Accrued Expenses are the total of unpaid bills outstanding at 31st March. The figure represents expenses that have been incurred during the year but not yet paid. The appropriate adjustment in the accounts is to Increase the relevant expense, e.g. Telephones, in the P/L account (DR), and create a liability in the Balance Sheet (CR) to show that the sum is unpaid--as an "Accrued Expense".

v) Prepayments are expenses paid in advance of the period to which they relate, typically for such items as Insurance. Only those expenses incurred during the year can be charged to the P/L account. So any expense actually paid during this year but which relates to next year must be deducted from this year's expenses. The appropriate adjustment is to reduce the relevant expense, since it includes the amount prepaid (CR), and also create a debtor in the Balance Sheet (DR) under a separate heading of "Prepayments". This is because if the business ceased to trade on 31st March (the Accounting Date), then any prepaid expense would have to be refunded to the business, so the prepayment is treated as a debtor.

vi) Bad Debts have been explained in chapter 2. In summary a bad debt is an amount owing to the business for work done/goods supplied but which has not been and is not going to be paid. It therefore becomes an expense or cost to the business and must be written off.

vii) Depreciation of assets. As explained in chapter 3, this is a subject best left to your accountant to advise upon. Technically it represents the proportion of the value of a fixed asset that has been "used up" in the current period to help produce the profit for the year.

viii) VAT is ignored for the purposes of drawing up final accounts. It is money that "passes through" a business but is independent of its operation, since it does not "belong" to the business.

ix) Figures shown as deductions in accounts are always expressed in brackets.

x) A calculation resulting from a deduction in the left hand column is extended one line lower and is shown in the centre column ; ditto in the centre column is extended one line lower and is shown in the right hand column, if 3 columns are used.

A further refinement to the accounts can arise if a fixed asset is sold during the course of a financial year. The question that has to be decided is this.

Was it sold at a loss, in which case the proceeds of sale will be shown as an Expense, or did the sale generate a profit, in which case that profit is shown as Income. Calculating a profit or loss from the sale of a fixed asset is a matter best left to your accountant.

It is quite possible for a loss to be made on the sale of an old asset even though cash or a cheque will be paid into the business! It all depends upon the "Book value " of the asset at the time of sale, which again depends upon deducting the accumulated depreciation from its cost price. Suffice it to know that the sale proceeds must be accounted for in the P/L account.

No indication has been made in the illustration of taxation since the subject is beyond the scope of this book and to keep explanations as simple as possible. It should come as no surprise to learn that profits are taxed, after deducting all relevant allowances. The final accounts submitted to HMRC will normally accompany your personal Tax Return form, but again this is best left to your accountant. In any event, as a sole trader, or in partnership with others, you still have to pay NI contributions. These are recorded in a separate column, if you use a Single Entry cashbook system, or in a NI account if you use a Double Entry system.

A different layout of the Profit and Loss account for a small manufacturing business might appear as follows:

TURNOVER   x

Less cost of sales   (x)
= Gross profit

Less expenses
Distribution costs   x
Admin expenses   x
= Trading profit

NOTES:

i) Turnover means Sales Revenue net of VAT.

ii) Cost of Sales is the total of all costs associated with making the products sold in the period. These would include raw materials costs; wages and salaries of workers; an appropriate proportion of production overheads including factory/workshop costs, but would exclude the costs of unsold production i.e. stock.

iii) Distribution costs and administrative expenses are self explanatory.

It is useful to remind ourselves once again that all the items in the P/L account are Nominal Accounts, as first mentioned in chapter 3, i.e. accounts in name only, since they do not relate to "Real" tangible assets nor to "Personal" accounts, for persons.

THE BALANCE SHEET

Together with the P/L account, the Balance Sheet sets out in summary form the financial position of the business at the close of the financial year.

Like the P/L account, various methods of presentation layout are possible, though usually a three or four column vertical form is used to show the broad categories of information, as illustrated later in the narrative.

The "Capital Employed" by a business is the term used to describe and explain the value of the capital that is used to generate the profit or loss, as calculated and shown on the P/L account. It is conventionally shown under that descriptive heading, below which are the various categories of Capital utilised.

The other half of the Balance Sheet is set out under the descriptive heading entitled "Employment of Capital". This shows the areas of the business where the capital is utilised, e.g. how much capital is represented by Fixed Assets, and by Current assets, and by Work-in-progress, etc. etc. Also shown is the money owed to the business and how much the business owes to its creditors.

The terminology used suggests that the total value of Capital Employed must equal the total value of the other half of the Balance Sheet equation, Employment of Capital. If this is not the case, then the Balance Sheet will not balance, which means that an error or series of errors has occurred in the calculations.

Errors could occur literally anywhere, in any account or a series of accounts.

Considering that the Balance Sheet is the culmination of a whole financial year's bookkeeping, it is a timely reminder of the importance of regular and accurate book-keeping and the production of frequent trial balance exercises.

If for example monthly trial balances have been drawn down accurately for the first ten months of the financial year, then it follows that any errors must have occurred in the final two months. In most cases this will be so. But there remains one other area of potential error and that is the figure calculated for Profit or Loss for the year. This figure is carried forward from the P/L account to the Balance Sheet because it represents an addition to Capital Employed, if a profit, or a reduction to Capital Employed in the case of a Loss. If that figure is wrongly calculated then the Balance Sheet wont balance, so it is good practice to check it first.

As a matter of form it does not matter whether "Capital Employed" is set out before or after "Employment of Capital".

Either method of presentation is acceptable, although the more modern form is to show "Employment of Capital" first, followed by "Capital Employed". This will be the format followed in our illustration. We will recall that the categories of account appearing in the Balance Sheet are the Assets and Liabilities of the business.

A) ASSETS.

These include all the items of value owned by the business, including what is owed to it. Each is shown in one of two categories as follows:

i) **Fixed Assets.** Those with a relatively long life which are used on a continuing basis in the activities of the business and are sometimes referred to as Tangible assets. They include freehold premises, the value of a leasehold, furniture, motor vehicles, machinery and equipment.

ii) **Current Assets.** These are Cash or other assets expected to be converted into cash in the near future. It is an accounting convention to show them in increasing order of "liquidity", ie the ease with which they are convertible into cash, the least liquid being shown first, as follows:

a) Closing Work-in-progress and/or Stock are the least liquid because you don't know when they will be converted into cash by sales.

b) Next comes Debtors (customers who have yet to pay for goods/services supplied), sometimes shown as Amounts due from Customers/Clients. From this sum will be deducted any amount assumed to be Bad Debts.

Note that if a "Bad Debt" does get paid later, an adjustment must be made in the subsequent year's Balance Sheet.

c) Next in order of liquidity will be payments made in advance, or Prepayments. Think about this from the "snap shot" viewpoint, which is what the Final Accounts represents. A payment made in advance is a kind of "loan" and a refund would be due should trading cease at the end of the accounting period.

Therefore it is an asset. Prepayments occur because financial periods for your insurers, for example, do not necessarily coincide with the financial year of the business, so overlap payments often occur if such payments are required in advance.

d) Next in order of liquidity is Cash at the bank.

e) Finally the most liquid of all assets is Cash in hand, represented by Petty Cash, accounting for which will be dealt with in chapter 6.

B) LIABILITIES

From the aggregate total of Fixed and Current assets must be deducted the total Liabilities of the business at the "snap shot" date, i.e. the monies owed by the business.

i) **Current Liabilities.** Are those debts which fall to be paid within the coming 12 months. These include:

a) Bank Overdrafts

b) Trade Creditors

c) Outstanding expenses. These are running costs not yet paid, otherwise known as Accruals or Accrued expenses.

ii) **Long term Liabilities.** Those debts falling due for settlement 12 months or more after the date of the Balance Sheet. Such liabilities are usually long term loans but exclude bank overdrafts, which can be called in at short notice at any time.

A typical Balance Sheet layout looks as follows:

Employment of capital

£

£

Fixed Assets
Land and building at cost
Fixtures and fittings at cost   Less
accumulated depreciation
Motor vehicles at cost
Less accumulated depreciation

CURRENT ASSETS
Closing work in progress
Debtors
Less provision doubtful debts
Prepayments
Cash at bank
Petty cash

LESS CURRENT LIABILITIES
Bank overdraft
Creditors
Accrued expenses

NET CURRENT ASSETS

LESS: LONG TERM LIABILITIES
Bank loan

REPRESENTED BY
Capital as at 1st April (same year)
Add net profit for year
Less: drawings from the business

Notes:

i) Deductions are again always shown in brackets;

ii) A calculation resulting from a deduction in the left-hand column is extended one line lower and shown in the centre column; ditto in the centre column is extended one line lower and shown in the far right hand column.

Another purpose of the Balance Sheet is to provide a basis for valuing the business as an entity. Taken literally, a Balance Sheet is a sheet of the balances taken from the double entry system of bookkeeping at the end of a financial year.

But the values shown are probably not what the business is worth. This value would reflect the subjective judgement of a potential buyer, considering his/her estimation of the market value, perhaps building in an allowance for "goodwill", i.e. the value attaching to the name and reputation of the business. Also the asset valuation method used by a buyer is normally based on present market values, not the historical cost of the assets used in arriving at the book values.

As we have seen, the principle of Double Entry provides that in the Balance Sheet the total Assets must equal the total Capital.

The total Capital is another way of describing the sources of finance used in a business, which is another way of describing what is owed by the business to those providers of the finance.

Let us examine the Sources of finance available to a business. These consist of:
a) Current liabilities owed to creditors, i.e. debts due for settlement within 12 months (money owed to creditors does not belong to the business but is used by it); and

b) Long term liabilities, i.e. debts due for settlement 12 months or more after the end of the financial year; and

c) Capital provided by the owner(s) of the business. Capital represents your personal financial interest, i.e. what the business owes you.

The logic of the Double Entry system dictates that:

* An increase/decrease in the value of an asset must be matched by either

i) An increase/decrease in a Source of Finance (a liability); or

ii) An increase/ decrease in the value of another asset.

* An increase/decrease in a Source of Finance must be matched by either

i) An increase/decrease in the value of an asset or

ii) An increase/decrease in another Source of Finance

Finally, remember that a Balance Sheet can be struck at any time, not just at the year end, though generally speaking it is only left until then.

5

Accounting for Petty Cash

Small Cash payments will need to be made in the day-to-day course of business. Accordingly it is necessary to record these payments separately from the main cash account because:

i) they are made in cash;
ii) being small sums it is easier to lose track of how much has been spent and on what;
iii) they are business costs like any made by cheque and must be accounted for as expenses.

A word of warning. If cash sales are made in the course of business DO NOT account for them in the petty cash accounts. Sales are NOT to be confused with minor expenses.

Mixing the two kinds of cash is not uncommon in cash-based businesses, but it is a fundamental error of principle and practice.

Always record petty cash expenditure as it is incurred, preferably by the use of pre-printed vouchers. You also need a ready-ruled Petty cash accounts book to compile the account from the vouchers. Both can be bought from your business stationers.

In the normal course of events you always carry some cash with you, going about your personal daily affairs. Sometimes you will be going about the affairs of the business at the same time and will need to distinguish the following occasions when you spend cash:

a) On the business premises
From time to time you will need postage stamps, biro pens, packets of envelopes, tea, milk, coffee, etc. and cash can be used from your Petty cash box for these purchases.

Even if you use your own money you must still record the purchase on a voucher and reimburse yourself from the petty cash box, because the business owes that money to you.

b) On your travels

All money spent by you in the course of business is a legitimate business expense, because it comes from business funds and therefore "belongs" to the business, not to you personally.

Get into the habit of asking for receipts for small sums spent and staple each receipt to a voucher. With or without receipts, total up the sum spent, on a weekly basis, and write a business account cheque to yourself for the amount expended from your personal funds.

Typically purchases will be for such items as petrol, parking meters, railway tickets, mini-cab fares and perhaps telephone calls made out of the office, e.g. from home. Some of these examples will generate receipts, some not. In all case, if you are registered for VAT (see chapter7) you must record the VAT separately, because it will be recoverable. (Remember that stamps and food items do not carry VAT).

Petty Cash Exercise for Helen (t/a Helen's Fashions)

At the end of a busy week Helen, (trading as Helen's Fashions) took the following receipts for various purchases from her bag and from the glove compartment of her car:

	£
Petrol	15.20
Buttons	6.75
Lunch (with Susan Jones)	27.75
Phone Cards	8.00
Rail Ticket	14.30

Her diary for that week showed that Helen had spent further small sums without obtaining receipts:

Parking meters	3.50
Telephone calls (coins)	1.20
Trade Newspaper	2.60
Tea, sugar, milk	4.95
Mini-cab fares	6.00

Notes:

i) Helen is to be commended for being a methodical and disciplined businesswoman.

ii) Lunch expenses with Susan Jones. Business entertainment expenses are not tax deductible unless Helen can prove to HMRC that they led to her obtaining business outside the U.K.

If the lunch did lead to an export deal she has a prima facie case for claiming it as an allowable business expense.

An exception arises in the provision of Xmas lunches/drinks for employees, where HMRC allow a modest sum for the "Xmas bash". Check the current limits with your accountant since Tax legislation changes every year.

How much Petty cash should be kept in the business? By implication (and for security purposes), such sums should be small, to cover say 1-2 weeks average weekly spend.

The recording system

The most common form of Petty Cash control is called the Imprest System, which works in the following way.

Having decided on, say, £50 as a comfortable and realistic "float", draw this sum from the business bank account by cheque. During week 1 assume say £38.50 is spent, leaving £11.50 in the box. At the start of week 2, draw out by business cheque a further sum of £38.50, bringing the petty cash float back up to £50.

The Imprest system can be checked at any time. Cash in hand plus the amount detailed on petty cash vouchers (for cash spent) for the period should always total £50.

As mentioned, a pre-printed Petty Cash book is the most sensible method for permanently recording how much has been spent and on what. Analysis columns will enable you to categorise expenses in the same way that major expenses are detailed in the Analysed Cashbook.. If you intend to use the Double entry system you will need to complete the double entry of expenses and receipts.

As we already know the Bank Statement will show a DR entry for the cash withdrawn. Therefore the Cash Account will record a CR as the corresponding entry. Therefore the Petty Cash Receipt entries will represent the DR entries of the internal Accounting system. The corresponding CR entries are therefore the expenses columns in the Petty Cash book, summarised first in the Totals column

To finalise the double entry, add up each expense column and enter this sum as a DR on the relevant "main" account. So for example the amount for petrol can be DR-ed to the Travel Expenses Account, and likewise for all other petty cash disbursements.

6

Accounting For VAT

A fully comprehensive guide to the complexities of the VAT system is beyond the scope of this book and only a brief outline will be provided. Suffice to say that if you are registered for VAT with HM Revenue and Customs then you are liable to account to that authority for VAT passing through your books. In effect you are an unpaid tax collector.

Your local VAT office will advise you on all VAT matters and enquiries regarding VAT administration. Do not neglect to seek advice from R and C and/or your accountant before you commence business, because:

a) the best advice will depend upon the circumstances of your business; and

b) you will not be excused by HM Revenue and Customs for failing to get advice. They will presume you have been so advised on how the system works and what you have to do; and

c) the system is complex.

The VAT system

Value Added Tax is defined as the tax chargeable on the supply of goods or services, where the supply is a taxable supply and made by a taxable person in the course of business carried on by him/her. The taxable person is s/he who is liable to account to HM Revenue and Customs for the amount of tax charged on the supply of goods/services.

A "Business"

When are you in business and when are you not?

"Business" can have a very wide meaning and includes the way in which self-employed individuals earn income by way of trade, vocation or profession.

HM Revenue and Customs define business as "any continuing activity which is mainly concerned with making supplies to other persons for a consideration".

Supply of Goods

This means a supply that transfers the exclusive ownership of the goods to someone else.

Supply of Services

This means doing something (except supplying goods), and receiving in return what the law calls a "consideration". This means any kind of payment - monetary or otherwise, and includes something which is also a supply. So a "consideration" to the business in return for the business making a supply includes anything given to cover the costs of making the supply.

Taxable Supply

This means any supply of goods/services except an exempt supply. Exempt supplies are listed in Schedule 6 of the VAT Act 1983 and include insurance, financial and postal services, and health services.

Taxable supplies are of two kinds:

i) Those chargeable at the Standard rate (currently 15% at time of writing).
ii) Those chargeable at a zero-rate. Zero rated supplies include books

and periodicals, and food not consumed on premises but which is sold for outside consumption.

Exempt and Zero-rated supplies are similar because no VAT is actually charged in either case to a customer.

However, you must be aware of the crucial difference between the two because only a registered business that makes a Taxable supply can reclaim VAT paid for supplies to that business. Zero rated supplies are taxable supplies. If your business makes Zero rated supplies it is a "Taxable Person" for VAT purposes. This means that VAT can be claimed back on purchases made by a business that is zero rated, if it is registered.

Exempt supplies are **not** taxable supplies. If your business only makes Exempt supplies it is not a "Taxable Person" for VAT purposes and therefore VAT paid on purchases by the business cannot be reclaimed from HM R and C.

There are special and complex rules about partial exemption applicable to suppliers of exempt goods/services (health operations, financial services and a few others). If you believe your business might qualify then contact your local VAT office. Briefly the size, type and level of business determine whether your business qualifies for partial exemption.

It should be clear by now that VAT can apply to your business even if the turnover is quite modest, because it is inevitable that VAT is going to be paid on purchases, regardless of whether it is charged on sales.

Discounts on Taxable Supplies

If you intend to offer discounts on products or services, as many businesses do, you need to know the VAT position on this kind of sale. There are two kinds of discount in operation in business.

a) An unconditional discount to a customer naturally means that s/he will pay the asking price less the discount. VAT is charged on the lower price because that is the asking price, the one the buyer will accept.

b) A conditional discount is one where a lower price will operate provided that the buyer pays promptly within a specified discount period, e.g. 14 days. In this case VAT is charged on the lower, discounted sum even if the customer does not pay within the specified discount period.

The tax value of the supply is the value of what is provided on which VAT is charged, because the lower sum will be at least the minimum amount paid for the purchase, assuming that the buyer takes advantage of the discounted price.

Time of Supply

The time at which a supply is made is known as the Tax Point. It is important because it begins the period at the end of which a taxable business becomes liable to account for tax charged on a taxable supply.

Generally the Tax Point for the sale of goods is when the goods are given over to the purchaser, which of course may not be when they are paid for, as in a credit sale.

The Tax Point for services is when the services are completed, which again may not be the same time as when they are paid for.

The most important exceptions are:

i) If a tax invoice is issued within 14 days after the basic tax point, the invoice date will be the tax point for the purpose of fixing the beginning of the quarterly period of account in which the VAT on it becomes liable for payment to HM R&C, unless a longer period is agreed.

ii) If payment is received, or a tax invoice rendered before the basic tax point arises, then the supply will be treated as occurring at the date the payment was made, or the date the invoice was rendered.

REGISTRATION

A) Compulsory
If you anticipate that the sales income of the business in the current trading year will reach the threshold level prescribed by law, you must contact your local VAT office and inform them that the business is liable for registration for VAT.

Upon registration the business will be allotted a unique Registration number, which must be shown on all business stationery.

VAT must then be charged on all sales the business makes, whether on credit or for cash, at the prescribed rate, except on those goods/services which are either zero-rated or exempt. This is called the Output Tax.

The VAT paid by the business on purchases of materials etc. is called the Input tax.

HM R&C must be paid the amount of VAT charged by the business on sales (**whether collected within the relevant quarter or not**) minus the VAT paid by the business on its purchases. This is normally done at the end of each quarter, though a longer time period can sometimes be negotiated.

Retail businesses, i.e. those selling to the public, do not need to render VAT invoices unless a buyer requests one.

HMRC publish a number of leaflets and notices explaining in great detail all you need to know about VAT and your business, as a sole trader, partnership or limited company.

Among the most important are:

I) VAT Notice 700: The VAT Guide. In fact a booklet of more than 140 pages.

ii) "Should I register for VAT?". This Guide is vital because HM R&C will impose financial penalties for failure to register when you should and also for late payments.

If you are fairly confident that within the next 30 days your taxable turnover for the past 12 months will exceed the threshold limit, then you must inform HM R&C.

iii) "Filling in your VAT Return". A useful guide on what format to adopt and how to present VAT Return forms.

If you believe that you are not obliged to register, because turnover will remain below the threshold, you should still consider the issue carefully. There are circumstances when you can reclaim VAT incurred before registration, if you then register at a later date. For example, VAT paid on vans (but not cars) and stock can later be reclaimed, disregarding the time of purchase, so long as the items are for business use. Of course you must produce VAT invoices to evidence the amount reclaimed.

If you engage the services of either solicitors or estate agents to set up the business, then VAT on their fee invoices can be reclaimed if they were incurred up to 6 months before the business was registered.

b) Voluntary
Compulsory registration arises simply because of the proximity of your turnover to the threshold level.

As an alternative you may want to consider voluntary registration, even if your turnover is substantially below the threshold level for compulsory registration.

The advantage is of course that Input tax paid on purchases subject to VAT can then be reclaimed.

The disadvantage is that VAT will have to be charged on the taxable supplies made by the business, which could well affect the competitiveness of your products/services. If competitors are not charging VAT and you are this might present a serious problem.

If the business is not registered, compulsorily or voluntarily, then it will have to bear the incidence of Input tax paid. You will have to consider whether the business can absorb this cost or whether you need to raise the selling prices.

Tax Invoices

A) Inputs to the Business

Once registered tax invoices are important because they evidence your right to recover Input tax on supplies made to the business by a supplier who is also registered. Without tax invoices you will not be able to claim a deduction of the VAT paid.

B) Outputs of the Business

If you have registered the business then you are compelled to charge VAT on sales, whether on credit or for cash.

Furthermore, tax invoices can only be raised if the business is VAT registered, and not otherwise.

As a matter of good business practice it is best to quote a VAT-inclusive price to customers. The current rate is significantly high and could have a serious impact on the cash flows of your own business and that of your suppliers, because most registered persons and businesses are locked in to the quarterly Return cycle.

Assuming the business is registered, and is therefore a taxable person, then within 30 days of making a physical taxable supply, the customer must be provided with a tax invoice.

Every Tax Invoice must by law state the following particulars:-

a) An invoice number, for identification purposes

b) The date of the supply, ie the tax point

c) The name, address and VAT registration number of the business

d) The name and address of the person to whom the sale has been made

e) The kind of supply that has been made, e.g. sale, hire

f) An adequate description of the goods or services supplied

g) The precise quantity of goods supplied or the extent of the services provided and separate amounts payable under each heading

h) The total amount payable and a breakdown of separate amounts against each item, if more than one

i) Details of any discount allowable for prompt cash payment

j) The rate of tax applicable and the amount of tax charged.

An exception applies to the "bottom line" value of a tax invoice if the VAT inclusive total is less than £100. If this is so you do not need to show VAT as a separate calculation but can instead show the one grossed up sum on an abbreviated tax invoice. It is important to get all this information correct on all output invoices and also to check that it is right on input invoices.

If upon inspection invoices do not satisfy HMRC requirements then you put at risk your ability to reclaim input tax. Bear in mind that HMRC have authority to inspect all your books and records relating to VAT at any time, with or without your co-operation.

An additional aid to VAT invoice monitoring is a simple invoice book, listing all invoices raised in number sequences and with separate analysis columns providing for arithmetic calculation of output VAT and net sales.

Tax collection

As noted previously, accounting for VAT is almost always to quarterly accounting periods. With permission from HMRC you may want to opt for an annual accounting scheme, where one tax return is made at the end of the year and the tax liability paid by direct debit in nine monthly instalments of amounts agreed with the CE.

Within one month after the end of a tax quarter, a completed return form and a cheque for the tax due must be sent to HMCE. There are penalties for late payment.

The Statutory return form provided by your local VAT office must detail the amount payable and how that sum has been calculated, i.e., the total output tax charges less the total input tax deductible. The return must also detail the VAT exclusive values of all sales and purchases made and incurred. The leaflet accompanying the form shows you exactly how to set this information out.

Bad debt relief

As noted previously, it is possible that your business will incur a bad debt, from time to time. The amount to be written off can include VAT if the invoice raised was a VAT invoice. Relief can be claimed for the VAT element of a bad debt which is more than six months old and has been written off in your accounts. If the debt is subsequently paid then naturally you must refund the VAT portion of the debt, whether recovered in whole or in part.

Accounting for VAT in your books

You are required to keep records of all taxable supplies and receipts of taxable goods and services made in the course of business. This includes standard, zero rated and exempt supplies.

If your methods of keeping these records create problems for HMCE in any audit exercise they carry out they have power to direct necessary changes to your procedures.

All VAT records must be kept for six years and can only be disposed of with the permission of HM R&C.

We have already examined how to highlight the VAT element in your book of accounts.

a) The single entry analysed cash book system
On both the receipts and payments side of the cash book, identify the VAT element and the net amount by using separate analysis columns for each.

b) The double entry cash account system
A separate VAT/HMCE account is maintained, as for any other type of account, to record movements of VAT.

7

Bank Reconciliation's

The purpose of Bank reconciliation's is to match what the bank statement shows as being in the business bank account at the end of an accounting period (usually a month), to what your books of account show as the position. In other words a reconciliation exercise of the external control of the business to the internal control system, i.e. the Cashbook or the Cash Account.

It is essential to conduct bank reconciliation exercises on a regular basis because it is an effective way

i) to assess the accuracy of your book-keeping; and
ii) to compare the financial state of the business with an external reference, which operates to monitor the behaviour of the business.

Discrepancies between the monthly closing balances of the cash book/cash account and the bank statement will inevitably occur because of the time lags in the processing and recording of monies paid in to the bank.

A bank reconciliation statement should be set out methodically and follow a simple system of recording discrepancies. The reconciliation statement should start with the balance according to the bank statement. Adjustments are then made by listing all the items which have not been entered in either set of books at the relevant date. A balance is then struck at the end of this arithmetic exercise showing the true position of the account, both internal and external balances being the same.

The reasons for the time lags that produce the overall discrepancy between the two accounts include the following:

i) Cheques may have been drawn and the payments entered in the appropriate internal books or on the payments side of the cash book, but not yet cleared through the banking system. Cheques can take between 3 to 5 working days to clear the system, depending on whether they are drawn on one of the four clearing banks, or on a smaller bank or Building Society account.

If a cheque drawn on your business account does not appear on the bank statement it is "unpresented".

The appropriate adjustment is to add the payment-out to the DR side of the bank statement, thus decreasing the balance if in credit, or increasing an overdraft, if shown.

ii) Receipts recorded in your books may have been too recent to have been cleared by the bank. Such cheques may have been banked at a different branch to your own, or they may reflect cash/cheques received but not yet banked.

The appropriate adjustment is to add the receipts to the CR side of the bank statement, thus increasing the balance if in credit or decreasing an overdraft, if shown.

iii) DR items may appear on the bank statement but not in the cash book. Examples include:

a) Bank charges debited automatically by the bank for operating the account;

b) Standing Order payments - regular payments to the credit of others and paid by the bank on your instructions e.g. business rates;
c) Direct debits - charges automatically made on the account by another person, though with your authority e.g. insurance premiums.

The appropriate adjustments for all of these is the same as in (i) above. Reduce the balance in the cash book/cash account by way of a CR entry or an entry in the payments side of the analysed cash book.

iv) CR items may appear on the bank statement but not in the cash book/cash account. This can happen if a debtor pays one of your invoices by instructing his/her bank to credit your bank, rather than posting the cheque to you.

The appropriate adjustment is the same as in (ii) above. Increase the balance in the cash book/cash account by way of a DR entry .
v) It is uncommon but not unknown for banks to make errors in preparing bank statements. Such errors will become apparent in the process of reconciliation.

vi) It is likewise not unknown for bookkeepers to make errors of the kinds explained earlier. Again these will be revealed in the reconciliation process.

Before drawing up the reconciliation statement the following steps are advisable.

First tick off all payments and receipts in the cash book/cash account with all the corresponding items on the bank statement.

Then enter into the cash book/cash account all bank charges, direct debits, standing orders and interest receipts and tick off those. Any remaining unticked items must therefore be un-presented cheques or late credits. Make a list of each and draw up a reconciliation statement in the following format, using the bank statement as the "control" account.

This illustrates the situation where the bank statement shows a CR closing balance, that is the account is in credit.

If the closing balance shows an overdraft then to calculate the true position the procedure shown above must be reversed.

Starting with a DR balance at the bank as the closing balance, unpresented cheques must be added, since they will increase the DR figure.

Likewise, late credits must be subtracted since they reduce the amount owed to the bank.

The format used can be varied, but so long as the principles are understood and applied then the two balances should be reconciled with little difficulty.

Section 2

Formulating Budgets and Controlling Cashflows

8

Budgets and Cash flow generally

Accurate forecasting, through the formulation of budgets and monitoring of cash flow is absolutely essential to the profitability of any business. In the previous chapters, we have seen how to develop and maintain books of account. In the following chapters we will look more closely at the process of budgeting in small businesses and at more precise control of cashflows.

Profitability of a business is the outcome of two elements

- control of overheads
- correct pricing to ensure that the margin of profit is realistic.

Cash flow

A smooth and regular cash flow, or the achievement of such involves:

- Making sure that a business is run profitably
- Payment control
- Utilisation of any available credit. This is of the utmost importance as the alternative is costly borrowing
- The attainment of correct stocking levels

Basically, money is vital to the life of any business and the forecasting of cash flow is essential in order to both measure the growth and direction of the business and to enable you to make strategic decisions at a given point in time. It is equally vital to ensure that sources of business finance are identified and readily available in times of increased need for capital.

Budgets

A budget is used, in both business and personal senses, as a tool to forecast expenditure and to monitor cash flow at regular intervals. It is a plan expressed in quantitative terms and should be part of an ongoing business plan. Budgets are necessary to enable you to plan what your business will do at given points of time. All aspects of a business have to be defined and factored into a budget, which will usually run for the financial year of the business and be broken down into monthly elements in order to allow for an ongoing review of progress. An effective budget is also essential as a tool to enable you to deal with potential funders, such as bank managers.

The monitoring function of a carefully prepared budget can help you to identify certain trends and needs, such as the maintenance of stock levels, debtors, creditors and suppliers generally. We will be looking in more depth at these processes further on in the book.

An effective budget is both a guesstimate and, in certain areas, an accurate appraisal of expenditure.

Formulating budgets

Whilst accounts show what has happened over a predetermined period of time, the budget will, or should, show what will happen in the near future. Budgets are essential tools in forecasting the pattern of business and also as a tool for development. For budgets to be of any real use they should be split up into monthly periods. As the months pass any adjustments can be made in the light of variations and can be fed into the ongoing budget. The putting together of a detailed budget involves a process which is linked. Key links in the budget setting process are outlined below:

• Sales budget-production budget

You need to consider the production capacity when setting the sales budget. It is essential that accuracy is achieved in this area as it is no good budgeting for production of goods which exceeds your real capacity.

- Sales budget-cost of sales

There are close links between these two budgets. The selling price has to reflect the costs of production and an element for profit. You will need an idea of the sales volume when setting this budget as the costs of production go down as actual production goes up.

- Overheads-sales budgets

The overheads of the business will be incurred whatever the level of turnover. However, the cost of the overheads will need to be carried by the sales of the product. The lower the volume of sales the more overhead cost has to be absorbed in the selling price of each item. In practice the overhead expenses are often apportioned back to the cost of sales on a cost centre basis. This is affected by the size of the organisation and its diversity.

All these elements grouped together will enable you to ascertain the budgeted gross and net profits for the period. In a small organisation the process of budgeting will be invariably easier as there will be less considerations. However, the larger and more departmentalised an organisation becomes the greater the need for co-operation between people and departments.

Cash flow considerations

Central to any budget setting is the need to estimate cash flow and to ensure that your projections are adequately sourced. It is no good having a production budget which anticipates an increase of 50% in production if the money is not there to finance it. We will be looking at cash flows a little later on.

As we have seen it is necessary to split the budget into periods of one month in order to account for variations or fluctuations in the process. This is very important if the nature of your business is affected by seasonal trends.

To re-cap, the key steps involved in budget preparation are as follows:

- The period that should be covered by your budget has to be ascertained. Usually, the period will correspond to the financial year of a business. It is also necessary to decide the periods into which the budget will be divided, i.e. 12 monthly periods

- Forecast activity levels and the income from trading and other sources for each of the periods. The forecast should reflect the fact that income streams may be irregular, as is the nature for some businesses

- When the level of sales has been determined for each period it is then necessary to ascertain the cost of sales

- The next step is to forecast the level of each of the overhead expenses.

- Finally, confirm that your plan fits into the cash budget.

Having arrived at the figures you will be in a position to produce a monthly budgeted profit and loss account like the one shown overleaf. The budget will have an actuals column and also a budget column. This will enable you to see, on a monthly basis, the level of expenditure and the deviation from the budget. If there are significant variations between the actual and budget column then there will be several considerations:

- It is essential to consider why the business is not performing as you have forecasted. Where are things going wrong, if they are going wrong

- The budget may need to be revised for the rest of the year, based on the variations, which may involve management decisions related to expenditure

As we will see, this procedure of review is extended automatically to the cash flow forecast.

There are key considerations for any one involved in budget setting. These are as follows:

- The quality and accuracy of any budget will depend on the assumptions made by the person/people involved in the budget process. Do not be sloppy and lazy when it comes to forecasting.

- Be rigorous and honest in your assumptions. The most important thing to realise when setting the budget is that, in a lot of cases, it will be essential to study the previous year's performance in order to be able to set a future budget.

- The budget is very much a management tool and the performance against budget at the end of each period is a crucial indicator for the future.

- Cash is the lifeblood-business activity totally depends on it and it is vital that this side is under control.

- The activities of one particular period in time will reflect and modify the next period.

Example monthly budgeted profit and loss account overleaf.

Example monthly budgeted Profit and Loss account

Items	January		February	
	Budget	Actual	Budget	Actual
Sales				
Direct costs				
Purchases of goods				
Wages				
Stock				
Cost of goods sold				
Gross profit				
Overheads				
Motor expenses				
Repairs and renewals				
Telephone charges				
Printing and stationary				
Heating and lighting				
Insurance				
Rates				
Bank charges and interest				
Professional fees				
Sundry expenses				
Depreciation				
Net profit				

The budget and its success will form your business model and should be treated with the utmost respect and consideration.

Budgeting and costs

The format of a budget should, broadly, follow the profit and loss account, although it will also include items of a capital nature. The preparation of any budget will usually be more detailed than the profit and loss account.

Costs involved in business

Some expenses in business are fixed and some are variable. There are also direct and indirect costs involved in the production process. Most direct costs are variable whilst the indirect costs are usually fixed. Direct costs are those associated with the production of the product itself whilst indirect costs are concerned with the overall running of a business.

Fixed and variable costs

If we look at the elements of fixed and variable costs, then it can be seen that raw materials to produce a product will be variable. The higher the level of overall activity the more variable the material costs. Energy for production will correspondingly vary as will transport. The logic is that the more that a business produces the more variable will the overall costs be.

However, other costs, such as rent or rates and business rates will not vary with the highs and lows of production. These costs will remain stable, they will be the same even if you did not produce a thing. The costs of salaries are fixed and identifiable and are therefore fixed.

Semi-variable costs

Some costs are not regarded as truly variable. Key examples may be labour and machinery. When production reaches a certain limit it may be necessary to take on more labour and invest in more machinery. This will obviously come into effect with increased production and this is why labour and machinery has to be identified as semi-variable in nature.

Particular attention should be paid to this area as incorrect forecasting can have a detrimental effect on business planning.

Selling expenses

The size of a sales force will clearly be affected by the levels of activity within the business. If interest is shown in a product then it may be necessary to increase your sales force, if appropriate. This is also a consideration to take on board.

Budgeting sales income

The top line on the profit and loss account is usually the sales income. Very often it is the sales figure that heads the budget and everything else is fitted in.

If you have been in business for a while then past trends can influence your future budget. It will be essential to look at the number of units sold and also the values of those units.

The unit values decided upon by yourself will very much reflect the type of business that you are engaged in. For example, a publisher would measure units in terms of individual books, a window cleaner individual houses and so on.

Who should carry out the sales forecasting

If you work alone then the answer is simple-you will do the forecasting. If the organisation is larger then all departments will usually have a hand in the forecasting process. It is absolutely essential that the process is well co-ordinated.

Creating the budget

From research carried out you have identified that the sales of your product will be along the following lines:

Product	Unit sales per month £
Books-paperback	750
Books-hardback	350

Magazines   450

The prices of the products are likely to be:

Books-paperback   7.99
Books-hardback   9.99
Magazines   3.50

Therefore the monthly sales figures would look like this:

Product	Units	Price £	Value £
Books-paperback	750	7.99	5992.50
Books hardback	350	9.99	3496.50
Magazines	450	3.50	1575
		Value	**11064**

If your business has seasonal trends then it will be necessary to produce separate figure for each month in order to maintain an accurate picture.

Arriving at price-price budgeting

You will usually have a keen idea of the market and corresponding prices for your goods. However, you also need to sell your goods at a profit and you therefore need to establish how much the product has cost in order to ascertain your profit margins.

When trying to establish the actual cost of production it is necessary to take into account the fact that there are two types of cost-direct and indirect costs. As we have seen, direct costs are those incurred directly in producing the product and they include materials, wages and other direct costs such as energy.

Indirect costs are those costs which do not relate directly to production, including costs of selling and marketing, rent, rates and insurance.

Example - Direct and indirect costs

Direct and Indirect costs

Direct Costs	Indirect costs
Materials	Overheads
+	Admin+labour
Direct Labour	Selling and marketing
+	Insurance-building repairs
Production costs	Depreciation

Proportion

COST OF ITEM

Having projected your sales and anticipated income, then you will need to set this off against the actual costs of production. Remember the actual cost of production will include all costs, direct and indirect. Therefore, if you are producing books, and you both manufacture and sell the product and the out turn price of a paperback is £7.99, this will be set off against the actual costs of production. For example:

Costs of production

Product-Paperback book

Print run 1000

Materials required

	£
Paper 100 mts	Cost 150
Cover film	Cost 100
Bar code	Cost 9.99
Glue	Cost 20.00
	Total 279.99

Labour
4 persons @ £9.87 per hour for 15 hours £140.05

Overheads		£
Rent	per annum	5000
Rates		842
Light		600
Heating		1200
Transport		12500
	Total	15152

Based on the production of 50,000 units per annum

0.30p per unit times 1000 total 300

Therefore total costs of production are:

£720.04 for 1000 print run or 0.72p per unit.

The cost of distribution, which is carried out by an independent distributor, represents 55% of cover price (£7.99) which is £4.39.

Costs of production @ 0.72 per unit plus £4.39 distribution costs represents a cost of £5.11. This represents a profit so far of £2.88 per unit. Other costs, if they exist are the costs of sales, such as advertising and marketing.

However, assuming there are no other costs of sales then the actual cost to the publisher is £5.11 set off against the selling price of £7.99. The differential £2.88 represents profit of around 27% which is a respectable return on capital employed.

The cost of production including distributors costs produces a profit margin of £2.88. This is based on you having established that the market will pay £7.99 for your books. However, there may be situations when you are faced with the need to reduce prices in the face of fresh competition and price cutting. It may be that your competitor has produced a range of books which are similar to yours and is selling them at £5.99. You can go two ways here- maintain your prices and leave it to the consumer to discriminate or re-examine your pricing.

Reducing your product to £5.99 would have the effect of a loss of £2 per item which, when worked back would entail a loss of approximately 90pence per unit. If you were not prepared to tolerate this loss, or were in a position where you could not lose such an amount of money, then hard decisions have to be made.

The overall costings would need to be re-examined to see if any extra savings could be made. For example, many overhead costs are fixed and an increase in overall production could reduce costs correspondingly.

Break even analysis

One technique widely employed in this situation is called break-even analysis. In the example of the book, not enough is lost, even with such a big price production by the competitor, to warrant the need for a break-even analysis. However, there will be situations depending on the nature of a business, where it will be necessary to establish at what point in production you reach a break even level.

As we discussed earlier, expenses can be split into fixed and variable costs. Fixed costs will include all the overheads such as rent and rates and insurance whilst variable costs are those incurred in production itself. The total costs of running the business are therefore the sum of the fixed costs and the variable costs during that period.

The more items produced, the higher the total cost but even if nothing is produced fixed costs will be incurred. Therefore, you will need to know the point of production at which you break even.

Calculating the break even point

Whenever you sell a product, part of the proceeds of sale will be used to meet variable costs-the costs of producing a specific item. The rest is applied towards the fixed costs and the remainder, if there is any, will be profit.

The remainder, the profit, is referred as the contribution from the sale of the product.

	£
If a product sells for	7.99
And the variable costs are	2.89
The contribution is therefore	5.10

This means that for every unit sold you will receive £5.10 towards the business. If the fixed costs are £450 per week and you have sold 200 units you will have received £1020 contribution from the sales and be in profit. If however, you sell 89 units in that week you will receive £453.90 which will meet fixed costs and leave you in a break even situation.

You therefore have established that you need to sell 89 units in order to reach a position where you have broken even. Any less and you will be in a loss making situation, any more and your profit margin will begin to increase. If as a result of reviewing your situation, you decide to reduce prices then you will need to revise your sales forecast

Internal budgeting-budgeting for expected overheads and capital items

So far we have examined the forecasting of the level of sales, the direct costs of the products and how to calculate the gross profit arising from selling products. We need now to look at the other expenses of the business.

Budgeting for overheads

We need to look at the indirect costs associated with business activity, more specifically overheads.

Overheads include:
• Rent and rates

- Salaries

- Stationary

- Telephone costs

- Travelling expenses

- Insurance

- Bank charges

- Entertaining

- Depreciation

- Accountancy, audit and legal fees

Rent and rates

If you are leasing a premises then the overheads associated with this are fixed and known, i.e. fixed annual rental, insurance, service charge if appropriate and business rates. If you own the premises outright then the costs will be minus rent. The only unforeseen costs associated with both leased and freehold property will be unexpected repair costs.

Salaries

Wages will include all other associated costs such as employers National Insurance Contributions, pension contributions if any and any other benefits. A global figure for the costs of labour has to be established. These costs can be easily understood throughout the year, as the only variation will be cost of living increases and the occasional increase in NI contributions.

Stationary

This particular item will cover all the costs of stationary throughout the business. It includes company letterheads, envelopes, copier paper and so on. This has to be seen against a backdrop of the previous year's expenditure and can be quite easily ascertained.

Telephone

There are two elements to telephone charges, telephone also including fax:

Rental
Quarterly line rental
Calls

This area also has to be measured against the previous year's expenditure. It is an area that will vary depending on the levels of business. The only constant is the fact that whether business rises or falls the level of telephone activity is likely to remain constant. If you are losing business, calls will be made to potential customers. If your business activity has increased then the phone is likely to be used more. A look at last year's quarterly bills and progress against budget should help you to arrive at a fairly accurate picture.

Travelling

This particular cost will vary widely from one business to another. Certain businesses require very little travel whilst others require extensive rail, air and road travel. Again, this cost will be influenced by the level of business and you should be able to ascertain the broad cost quite accurately.

Insurance

A business will need several different insurances. These include:

- Public liability

- Employers liability

- Building insurance

- Equipment insurance

- Consequential loss insurance

- Product insurance.

Obviously, the nature and type of your business will determine the types of insurance needed. These will be easily identified and the costs fixed.

Bank charges

Banks publish a list of their charges and they should be quantifiable. However, charges can be negotiated so there may be room for improvement in this area.

Entertaining

This particular item will vary depending on the nature and type of the business. Again, you know the needs of your business and the value of entertaining and the costs should be easily quantifiable.

Depreciation

This reflects the loss in the value of capital equipment. This is a revenue expense but has to be discussed further within the context of capital expenditure.

Accountancy and audit fees

The charges from your accountant can be fixed, i.e. one fee is payable or they can vary depending on the charging structure of the accountant used. In addition, the nature and type of service will vary, some companies will use an accountant for all its functions others will use them only for preparation of end of years accounts. Again, you know the extent to which accountants are used within your company and also the likely charges.

One other area to consider is that of selling and distribution and the expenses associated with these elements. These can include:

- Sales representatives salaries

- Commissions

- Travel expenses

- Sales office expenses

- Communications

- Accommodation

- Publicity (advertising)

And any other item associated with this area.

You should be in a position, having identified all the relevant cost areas to draw up an administration budget like the one shown overleaf.

Budgeting for capital items

The capital budget is every bit as important as the revenue budget. The revenue budget deals with the day to day running costs and income of the business, the capital budget will deal with the provision of capital items such as machinery, vehicles etc. The capital budget is of more relevance to cash flow than to revenue expenditure and we will be looking at this at little later.

Capital expenditure has an impact on profitability in two key ways:

- By increasing the depreciation charge

- By increasing the amount of interest payable as a result of borrowed money

The timing of capital expenditure can have a dramatic effect on cash flow of a business. It is important to time the acquisition of capital items with cash flow into the business as this will decrease reliance on the need to borrow or to spend much needed capital and find your business in trouble.

Example of an administration budget

Period 12 Months to 31st March

	Previous years actual
Current	
Budget	

Materials

Stationary
Other

Salaries and Wages
Management
Clerical
Cleaners
Other

Expenses
Rent and rates
Telephone
Postage
Travelling
Entertaining
Insurance
Bank Charges
Audit and accountancy
Subscriptions
Depreciation
Other

Example of an overall revenue budget

The period 12 months to 31ˢᵗ March

Products

	Type A	Type B	Type C
Total			
Sales			
Cost of			sales
Contribution to profit			
Selling and distribution overheads			
Administration overheads			
Total Overheads			
Budgeted profit			

9

Cash flow management

A cash flow forecast deals with transactions at the time of payment. Cash does not necessarily accrue at the same time as a sale takes place. The sale may take place in August of one year but, depending on what credit agreements you have in place with your customers, payments may arrive up to 3 months later. There are many stories of companies, particularly large companies, who withhold payments for 6 months or more.

Once you have prepared a budgeted profit and loss account it is then essential to review the cash situation of the business to ensure the finance will be there to make the business possible. Sales are the heart that pumps money into the business. Cash flow is payment for those sales, and this must be very closely regulated.

The cash flow forecast

Quite simply, a cash flow forecast will measure the flow and movements of cash. A bank will absolutely insist on seeing a well-prepared forecast. Most banks will provide a standard cash flow form like the one overleaf to assist those who are not so experienced in these matters. As with the budget, the actual timeframe covered by the cash flow forecast is very important. As with the budget, a cash flow forecast from month to month is the norm. This enables you to see the flow of cash in finer detail and enables you to plan.

If your business is of a certain type it might be possible to produce a cash flow forecast covering longer than the standard one-year period. This very much depends on your product and the nature of your sales. However, the longer a cash flow forecast covers the less accurate it is likely to be.

If you look at the standard cash flow form overleaf you will see that it is divided into the following parts:

- Dates covering the length of time relevant to the forecast

- Receipts

- Payments

- Opening bank balance

- Closing bank balance

The closing balance for one period will be the opening balance of the next period.

Looking at the headings on the form overleaf, it can be seen that income has been divided into:

- Cash sales

- Debtors

- Other income

Forecasting cash flow

The first heading, cash sales, entails sales where cash is received immediately. There is no credit period involved. Certain businesses are cash businesses. Shops, cafes, public houses are all in the position where they receive cash over the counter. This is as opposed to the business, which invoices for its sales. Cash includes cash, cheque, visa and so on. If you have a detailed monthly operating budget then it should be relatively easy to work out monthly cash flow.

Debtors

On a cash flow forecast we are concerned with cash transactions. The sale and when it is made is not relevant. This is more relevant to your operating budget. The most important entry will be the date that you expect to receive payment for that particular sale. This can be measured with some certainty by your agreed credit agreements with your customers.

The important thing is to monitor the cash flow on a monthly basis. It may well be that your customers will exceed the period of credit given to them and that you need to adjust your cash flow forecast as you go along.

The forecasting of other income

These entries will very much depend on the nature and type of your business. If you are VAT registered, and are fortunate enough to receive a refund then this will be a one off entry. There are a number of other items which may fit into this section, such as any loans given to the company by the owner, rent received from investments or finance from other sources.

Forecasting expenditure

The expenditure columns of the cash flow forecast are similarly divided into different sections. There are the cash purchases for those items where no credit is allowed, or no credit taken. There are creditors. This sum will represent those purchases where credit has been given. This sum will still have to be paid. This represents free finance and should be entered at the appropriate period when it is paid.

Salaries and wages and employers contributions

These expenses can be accurately predicted. The amount of PAYE will depend on the level of salaries and wages and will include

National Insurance and income tax. There may be other contributions depending on the nature of your business and the overall deal offered. Pensions may represent one such payment.

The timing of your PAYE payment is of relevance to your tax return. If the monthly value due to HM Revenue and Customs is less than a certain figure, currently £450, then it can be paid quarterly. If you exceed this amount then the payments must be made monthly. In both cases, the payments must be made on a certain date details of which can be obtained from HMRC.

Payments for use of energy

Payment for gas, electricity and any other energy sources will need to be included in this section. These payments will be almost certainly paid on a quarterly basis. Some companies, in particular those offering cheaper deals will sometimes insist on a monthly payment. This should be avoided if possible. There will be seasonal variations here, with winter costing more than summer and so on. These trends will have been recorded in your budget.

Payments for rent/service charge

Rental payments and other associated payments such as service charge and insurance payments for the building will normally be paid on a quarterly basis. It is highly unusual to pay these any more frequently. Rates due to the local authority will usually be made twice per year. However, this will depend on the local authority area and also your own agreement with them. It could be that you pay by monthly direct debit.

Bank and interest charges on overdrafts, loans and hire purchase

Bank charges will depend very much on how you manage your business and run your accounts. The more transactions the more the charges. You should be aware of the structure of charges, which relates to your particular bank and then you should analyse how you

10

Monitoring Budgets and Cash flow

Effective monitoring of budgets and cash flow entails regular scrutiny, the making of comparisons between what you have forecast and what is actually happening within your company.

On both the budget and cash flow there is a column entitled actual and projected. At the end of each given month it will be necessary to fill the actual column and measure this against expenditure and make appropriate revisions.

If things are seriously wrong then detailed analysis of your business activities is needed.

In many cases, there are crucial timing differences between income and expenditure which can cause problems. A typical budget and cash flow forecast, if all is going well will look like the example below. This is based on a publishing business, which has one month's credit with its suppliers and also gives one-month credit to its distributor. The unit cost is £7.99.

Monthly cash flow forecast
Sales

Budget	Jan	Feb	Mar	Apr	May
	2000	1500	3000	1750	2000
Sales value	15980	11985	23970	13983	15980
Purchases	7500	5625	11250	6562.5	7500

Overheads	1440	1080	2160	1260	1440
Profit	7040	5280	10560	6160	7040

The planned cash flow forecast should therefore correspond to the one below:

Cash flow	Jan	Feb	Mar	Apr	May
Income					
Sales		15980	11985	23970	13983
Expenditure					
Purchases		7500	5625	11250	6562.5
Overheads	1440	1080	2160	1260	1440
Surplus/ Deficit	-1440	7040	4200	11460	5980
Opening Balance		-1440	5600	9800	21260
Closing	-1440	5600	9800	21260	27240

If, however, your customer is one month late when paying a bill, this will throw your cash flow out and you will have to revise the columns accordingly. Those people who owe you money are called your debtors. Quite simply, they are in debt to you. It is vitally important that you maintain a system to monitor those who are in debt to you. Failure to do this will mean that you will be short of cash and your plan, based on your budget and your cash flow forecast, will not be accurate. It is best, when managing business, to have two sets of records for invoices, one for paid invoices and one for unpaid invoices. Those debtors who are late with payment are called "aged debtors" and the records kept by your self are called the aged debtors records. The analysis you carry out is called the aged debtor's analysis.

It is essential that you have a standard period within which you will send letters to debtors and a cut off period when you will take court action. Even if you pursue the customer for payment in the county court it is never sure that you will recover the debt. However, it is a matter of principle because cash flow management, as we have seen, is integral to your business.

Monitoring budgets

In addition to having to make adjustments to cash flow forecasts because of late payments and other reasons, it may be that you have overestimated your budget figures. In other words, you got the budget wrong. It is obviously very important to check the budget performance each month, i.e. budget against actual to make sure that performance in this area corresponds to your cash flow forecast.

Larger businesses will prepare a full set of operating accounts each month in order to ensure that they have an ongoing accurate picture. For small business, this is obviously impractical and therefore an ongoing monitoring of the budget and cash flow forecasts is crucially important.

One area which can potentially cause you problems is that of stock. The value of stock will often not vary from month to month though there may be seasonal trends. If the stock does vary a lot, and is giving cause for concern you have two alternative courses of action:

- Take stock each month and evaluate its costs

- Introduce a stock control system. This is the favoured approach as it is less time consuming. You record the amount of each line of stock on a separate account so that you can quickly evaluate its value.

Excessive stocks tie up much needed cash and will be a drain on your company's liquidity. There are a number of ways of deducing the amount of stock that you should carry. The important factors are:

- The amount of sales of that particular product

- Delivery times

- Discount policies on purchase

- The size of raw material batches ordered

- The value of the stock

You should be able to deduce an accurate stock level by looking at previous sales and the amount of stock consumed and projecting this forward to correspond to future sales. You will need a careful analysis of needs because obviously bulk buying at a discount will play a part. However, even if bulk buying, much needed capital could needlessly be tied up. The longer term cash benefits of discount must be weighed against ongoing sales and profit.

The use of financial ratios for monitoring budgets and cash flow

A financial ratio entails deducing the correlation between two figures and ascertaining the meaning of that correlation.

There are four types of financial ratios:
- Profit ratios - these show how efficient the business is, or how good it is, at making profit from capital invested.

- Efficiency ratios - these show the management efficiency of the business.
- Liquidity ratios - these ratios measure the working capital within the business

- Solvency ratios-they show how solvent the business is or how near it is to going bankrupt.

Profit ratios

There are three useful ratios, which indicate how profitable your business is:

- The gross profit margin
- The net profit margin
- The return on capital employed within your business

The gross profit margin

The gross profit margin is probably the most important ratio. The gross profit calculates the relationship between the gross profit and sales by the following method:

$$\frac{\text{Gross profit times 100}}{\text{Sales}} = \text{Gross profit margin}$$

The net profit margin

The net profit margin shows you the ratio after the deduction of all expenses of the business except tax. It is not as reliable an indicator as the gross profit margin but can be useful.
It is calculated as follows:

$$\frac{\text{Net profit times 100}}{\text{Sales}} = \text{Net profit margin}$$

The return on capital ratio

The return on capital ratio measures the revenue being generated from the capital employed in the business. This ratio enables you to compare the income produced by the business with income from other forms of investment. The ratio is calculated as follows:

$$\frac{\text{Profit before charging interest and tax}}{\text{Total capital employed}} = \text{Return on capital}$$

Efficiency ratios

Efficiency ratios divide into three areas each of which are further subdivided:

- Debtors
  Debtor's turnover ratio
  Debtor's collection period
- Creditors
  Creditors turnover ratio
  Creditors payment period
- Stock
  Stock turnover ratio
  Average stock holding period

The debtor's turnover ratio

These particular measurements show just how efficiently the capital utilised by the business is being used. The debtor turnover ratio shows the number of times that the unpaid debt is "turned over". It is calculated like so:

$$\frac{\text{Sales } (+ \text{ VAT})}{\text{Debtors}} = \text{Debtors turnover ratio}$$

The debtor's collection period

The debtor's collection period is a more useful ratio for measurement.

This shows the average number of days that it takes you to collect your debts:

$$\frac{\text{Debtors times 365}}{\text{Sales} + (\text{VAT})} = \text{Debtor collection period (in days)}$$

The creditors turnover ratio

You can check the creditors turnover ratio in a similar way and also the creditors payment period:

$$\frac{\text{Purchases} (+\text{VAT})}{\text{Creditors}} = \text{Creditors turnover ratio}$$

Creditors payment period

$$\frac{\text{Creditors times 365}}{\text{Purchases} (+\text{VAT})} = \text{Creditors payment period}$$

It is important to monitor the creditor period as well as the debtor's periods as you can run into trouble if you yourself become a debtor and run the risk of losing credit.

The final ratios here are the stock ratios. In the same manner as the ratios for debtors and creditors are measured, the stock turnover ratio and the average stock holding period can be calculated in the following way:

The stock turnover ratio

$$\frac{\text{Cost of sales}}{\text{Stock at cost}} = \text{Stock turnover ratio}$$

The average stock holding period

Stock at cost times 365

———————————————— = Average stock holding period

Cost of sales

Liquidity ratios

Important ratios for any business are those measuring liquidity. The following will be outlined:

- The current ratio

- The quick ratio

- The security interval

The liquidity ratios show the ability of the business to meet its liabilities as they fall due from its assets. A business should have sufficient current assets to cover its current liabilities.

The current ratio

The current ratio measures the ability of a business to achieve this, in this way:

Current assets

———————————— = Current ratio

Current liabilities

As discussed, current assets are items such as stock, work in progress, cash in the bank, debtors and cash at hand. Current liabilities are amounts owed by the business to its creditors and bank overdrafts. Current liabilities do not include items such as long-term loans, which do not normally fall due for repayment within 12 months. The current ratio will usually be between 1.5 and 2. If it is less than 1, you are probably relying on a bank overdraft secured on the long-term assets of the business, or delaying payments to your creditors. Whatever the situation, the requirement for working capital should be of some concern. If this ratio exceeds 2 then you may not be making the best use of your current assets. You may have too much cash in the bank or too much stock or to many debtors.

Checking the quick ratio

The current ratio checks all current assets and current liabilities. A better way, or test, is to check on those assets, which are cash, or near cash. This is the relevance of the quick ratio.

Assets such as stock and work in progress may be difficult to sell and covert into cash to pay the liabilities of the business and so these are excluded.

Only those quick assets that are left - cash, money at the bank and debtors, are included. The ratio is calculated as follows:

$$\frac{\text{Quick assets}}{\text{Current liabilities}} = \text{Quick ratio}$$

This ratio is usually between 0.7 and 1, although the nature of a particular business will affect this.

The security interval

This particular ratio measures how long the business could survive if no more cash was received but if it continued to pay its normal expenses. It is calculated as follows:

$$\frac{\text{Quick assets}}{\text{Operating expenses}} = \text{Security interval}$$

The security Interval is expressed as a daily figure.

This interval is usually between 30 and 90 days, although depends on the type of business.

Solvency ratios

There are two ratios in this group:

- The solvency ratio
- Gearing

If your total liabilities exceed your total assets then your business is technically insolvent. This is expressed as the solvency ratio, expressed as follows:

$$\frac{\text{Total assets of the business}}{\text{Total liabilities of the business}} = \text{Solvency ratio}$$

If this equation produces a ratio of less than 1 then you are insolvent. This is an are that you must keep under careful review, as you may reach a point when you cannot trade due to the inability to meet liabilities.

Even if the ratio is greater than 1, you cannot always feel totally secure. This is why the corresponding use of liquidity ratios is so important.

Checking gearing

The ratio of money that a business has loaned to the capital invested in the business by shareholders or the owners of the business is referred to as the gearing of the business. This includes accumulated profits if they have not been withdrawn. It is calculated as follows:

$$\frac{\text{Total borrowed}}{\text{Owners capital}} = \text{Gearing}$$

The gearing of a business is an important guide to how much the business should be allowed to borrow. In general, banks expect their lending to the business to be at least matched by the investment of the owners and shareholders. This means that a ratio

By using ratios you can check on trends and financial health of your business and also make a comparison with similar business as your own.

11

Using Technology

For a long time, the preferred method, through necessity, for the preparation of budgets and accounts for business was by maintaining ledgers by hand. This method has changed rapidly during through the introduction of either spreadsheets and/or computerised accounts packages. The spreadsheet is often the place where the company accountant rationalises the monthly profit and loss accounts and has become an indispensable tool for many businesses, both large and small.

Most businesses will use standard accounts packages and run these on systems running the Microsoft operating system. The most popular spreadsheet programme running under Microsoft windows is Excel which is a sophisticated package capable of catering for most of your requirements in presenting your profit and loss accounting. One of the main advantages to spread-sheeting is the ability to do 'What if?' scenarios on your accounts – for example by altering the sales figures up or down by a percentage you can instantly see the effect on the bottom line profit.

Using a spreadsheet

All spreadsheets are essentially the same. The origins of spreadsheets date from the accountants paper with its lines and columns. The main difference between spreadsheets and manually kept calculations is that a spreadsheet is maintained on a computer and the data is either input by hand, or transferred from your accounting package, with changes to all aspects of the spreadsheet calculations automatically happening when a figure is changed. For example, if a row of numbers adds up to a specific figure then a change to any one of those numbers will also change the bottom line instantly. The actual sheet on the computer screen is not simply one sheet of A4.

It is a large sheet, consisting of columns and rows. Usually there will be up to 256 columns and 8192 rows. The computer screen is a window which enables the user to focus in on a specific area of the spreadsheet.

Across the top of the worksheet are letters to identify the columns. These are A,B,C...X,Y,Z, AA, AB, AC...AX,AY,AZ, and so on.

Down the side of the sheet are the row numbers. In this way the sheet is divided into a maximum of 2,097,152 cells, each of which can be addressed by specifying the column and row number. Each cell on the spreadsheet can contain either data or a formula. The formula is quite often an instruction to add up or subtract and is linked from cell to cell.

Advantages of spreadsheets

There are many advantages of using a spreadsheet:

- Spreadsheets are easy to use

- Spreadsheets remove the need for endless calculations and can also remove much of the human error factor

- Budgets and forecasts are easy to modify on a spreadsheet enabling you to do 'What if?' analysis on your accounts.

Disadvantages of using a spreadsheet

You need to acquire a working knowledge of a spreadsheet so that you can utilise it effectively. Not everyone is computer literate and may find that they can more easily keep records manually

Sample Spreadsheet overleaf

	A	B	C	D	E	F	G
1	You can write your text across cells but it still 'belongs to cell A1 where you started					You can alter the width of columns	
2						using click and drag of column dividers	
3	Overheads						
4	Rent			Cell D3		⇐ Cell D3 down to	
5	Phone					cell D9 would	
6	etc.					contain number	
7						entries to be added.	
8							
9				Cell D9		⇐	
10							
11	**Total Overheads**			**= SUM (D3.D9)**		⇐ If a cell entry begins with the '=' sign then	
12	You can alter the depth of rows easily using click and drag of the lines					it will be doing a calculation depending on the function. The SUM function is common and adds the above numbers from D3 to D9	
13							

Workbooks

Each spreadsheet can further be incorporated into a workbook containing a number of spreadsheets and cell references passed across these spreadsheets. For example, as a small business you could keep note of all your paid invoices in one spreadsheet (say called paid invoices) which gives you a total of your monthly sales income. This cell (containing the monthly sales total) can be referenced from your balance sheet (a different spreadsheet in the workbook) such that much of the hard work of calculation is made easier.

You might also keep another spreadsheet for your monthly overheads – where many figures will be standard (unchanging) amounts – those overheads that change can be simply altered and the total again picked up in your profit and loss spreadsheet, providing you with instant changes and final results quickly.

See diagram overleaf

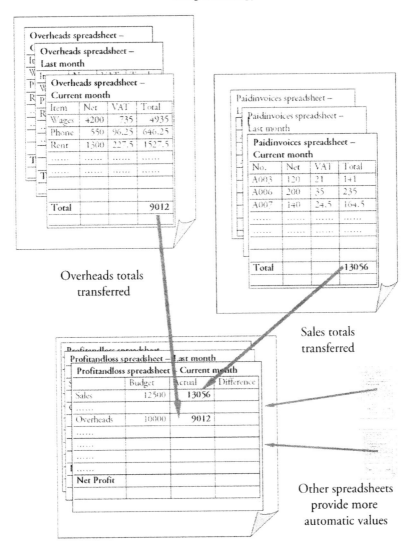

As you can see once you have entered your basic monthly sales figures, overheads, purchases, etc. all these figures are referenced from the profit and loss spreadsheet which largely creates itself from a standard template. Each month the new figures enable you to notice trends and changes which allows you to adjust budget figures accordingly for the coming months.

Although spreadsheets are wonderful for instant changes you do need to know what you are doing as one false move can produce errors that will affect final totals. However cells can be protected and entry limited so that it can be made foolproof for data-entry purposes. Templates can get extremely sophisticated these days and if you look on the web and google "excel accounts templates" for instance you will find many variations of templates on offer, some for free! This is a good way to start – this is a screenshot of a template downloaded from a Microsoft office site for expenses:

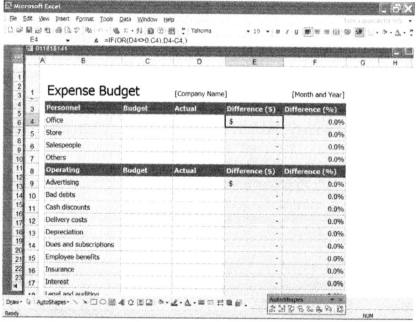

The Expense Budget template was downloaded from http://office.microsoft.com/en-au/templates/default.aspx. The template was one of many offered for free and is nicely formatted. Notice the cell referenced at E4 in the editing box above the function has a conditional reference =IF(OR(D4<>0,C4),D4-C4,) so that nothing is shown in this cell unless there is a figure in the previous column at D4 (actual value) – this shows some sophistication and by altering and adapting these templates you can both get a better view of your business and learn spreadsheeting at the same time.

A word of warning if you download these templates – always try to avoid disreputable sites as it is easy for trojans to creep into your system; always virus check downloaded files. Also be aware that not every balance sheet protocol of accounting is the same in every country. Apart from that they can provide a quick start to getting your accounts and budgets off the ground.

As you can see, the advantages far outweigh the disadvantages and it is rapidly becoming the norm for those who keep their own accounts to use a spreadsheet for management information. Many companies will use a standard accounting package to provide their monthly accounts – and indeed the better ones will provide instant profit and loss balance sheet. However, many accounting packages may lack the ability to account for certain aspects of your business and often the accounts department will have a method of transferring the essential information into a spreadsheet format for final preparation of accounts.

There are numerous courses available, low cost courses which can introduce people to spreadsheets and provide adequate basic training. The costs of packages now are low and any newly acquired computer will almost certainly contain a package, most often Excel, which comes with the Microsoft Office applications.

Glossary of terms

Accounting ratios
A set of ratios used to indicate a particular financial position of a company.

Aged debtors
This term is used to highlight those people who have been in debt for a longer period than the norm. It is normal practice to age debts in terms of months so that when a debt becomes a problem it requires chasing and settling.

Balance sheet
A statement of the worth of the business at the accounting date expressed in terms of historical cost.

Break even point
The point at which production equals the fixed cost-the point at which you break even.

Budgets
A financial/quantitative statement, prepared prior to an accounting period which forecasts future expenditure. The budget is used as a planning tool and is essential for the effective management of business.

Capital expenditure
Expenditure on fixed assets which have a lasting benefit to the business.

Cash flow forecast
A forecast showing the budgeted receipts and payments for the forthcoming year (or period).

Credit period
The period between the supply and invoicing of goods and services and the payment of the invoice.

Creditors
The suppliers to the business to whom money is owed and the amount owed by the business to them.

Current assets
These are assets which are either cash or can be turned into cash quite quickly. They include cash, bank balances, debtors. Stock and work in progress.

Current liabilities
These are amounts owed to suppliers (creditors) together with short term loans such as bank overdrafts,

Debtors
Those who owe money to the business

Depreciation
An allowance made for the reduction or dimunition of the value of fixed
assets.

Direct costs
Direct costs are those costs directly related to the production of the product.

Fixed assets
Property and equipment owned by a business which will have a long lasting benefit to the business.

Fixed costs
A fixed cost is a cost which is unaffected by variations in a firms production. A fixed cost may be rent, rates etc.

Gross profit
The profit earned by a business from trading, prior to the deduction of overhead expenses.

Indirect costs

Indirect costs are those costs which do not relate directly to the production of the product but are necessary to provide the setting within which the business is run.

Key ratios

Key ratios measure the performance of a business in a way that conventional analysis cannot. These ratios are essential to provide a picture of where the business is.

Long-term liabilities

Amounts owed by a business which are not due for payment within one year.

Net assets

Net assets are the total assets of the business minus its liabilities.

Net profit

The profit of a business after taking account of all its expenses.

Overheads

Money spent regularly to keep the business running. Overheads include rent, rates, salaries etc.

Profit and loss account

An account summarising the income and expenditure of a business for a given period and showing the surplus and deficit.

Quick assets

This is a subdivision of current assets, comprising assets which can realise cash quickly if needed.

Revenue expenditure

Revenue expenditure is wholly used up during the accounting period. Examples of revenue expenditure include raw materials, payment of rent and salaries.